Discourses
Volume Three
2016

DISCOURSES:
A True New Birth
Volume Three: 2016

Yogacharya David R. Hickenbottom

Editor: Ruth M. Lamb, Ph.D

The Cross and The Lotus Publishing
Camano Island, Washington, USA

Discourses—Volume Three 2016: A True New Birth
Copyright ©2023, The Cross and The Lotus Publishing

For permission requests, contact the publisher at:
http://www.crossandlotus.com/contact.html

ISBN: 978-1-957811-01-7 (softcover)
ISBN: 978-1-957811-02-4 (eBook)

All photos courtesy of Carla Hickenbottom Portfolio
unless otherwise attributed (see page 293)

Edited by Ruth Lamb

Book design by Jan Westendorp/Kato Design and Photo (katodesignandphoto.com)

Cover design by Rob Landers, Ruth Lamb, and Jan Westendorp

Printed and bound in the USA

Published by
The Cross and The Lotus Publishing
Camano Island, Washington, USA
Website: www.crossandlotus.com

Contents

OM TAT SAT AUM

Preface

Yogacharya David, Puri, India, 2013.

Life takes on an entirely new view when seen from the rear-view mirror, smoothing out bumps, soothing wounds, and clarifying lessons. What seemed an eternity of time then, seems only a blip on the screen now, remembered but pacified. One other thing: all of these experiences are now placed in a context of meaning that was often absent at the time. I see the great adventure of this life as refining and purifying consciousness, to make it ready for a true New Birth.

And this is the great lesson for me, from the time I was in my mother's womb until today. The meaning of life is found in the evolution of consciousness and its ultimate merging with Divine Consciousness.

It is finding union with the Divine that places all life-experience into its proper role. All life serves one ultimate, glorious purpose that makes it all worthwhile.

—YOGACHARYA DAVID

In *A True New Birth,* Yogacharya David takes us on a journey into life's deeper questions. Even while he is challenged by his own mortality during this year, Yogacharya David stays with the idea of the "holy breath," the notion that we are all living cathedrals. He affirms that humankind is to evolve as a race, and as a species, such that we gain the ability to raise the consciousness of this planet into the highest realms of Spirit. We begin with ourselves and then reach out to our homes and communities and onward to countries.

No matter what the situation, he affirms that we can find micro-moments of joy and "make a beautiful pearl necklace of God-Joy" as we string these moments together. He describes chanting as a route to this process. Yogacharya David suggests using the Aum/Amen chant as he says that this sound and force and frequency emanate from the creative principle from which all manifestation comes—hence, Divine Consciousness, the source of all that is. So, chanting the Aum can take the mind back to Source, to Spirit, and thereby enhance those micro-moments of joy. Even when moods fiercely track and trigger the psyche, joy can overcome! And to sustain the joy, seek service to the infinite through the thousands of opportunities that lovingly present themselves each day.

Yogacharya David assures us that all one needs is a willing heart to build a closer connection with the Universal Spirit that is all-pervading, the Spirit that includes material creation and all within and beyond.

While we can expect to be tested in the fires of the pure Light of Divine Consciousness, our reward is a deeper connection with the untold blessings that come with the inner sacred attunement we can develop with our unique soul-force. So, see clearly when the dark clouds of ignorance and maya and sneaking despair attempt to block the pure sun—stop the dark-process and chant God's name. Om Sri Ram, Jai Ram Jai Jai Ram—or affirm a chant that has purity and force, one that empowers your soul.

Yogacharya David reminds us in *A True New Birth* that God is working through us as we evolve to become sincere and conscious instruments in the hands of the Divine.

This volume teaches us to discern the difference between a free consciousness and a bound one—we can ascertain just what kind of steward we wish to be for ourselves and for the purpose we came to fulfil. Yogacharya David reminds us that our Spirit is great—" so great that it can reach out to the infinite."

A True New Birth is the third in a six-volume series of Discourses offered by Yogacharya David between 2013 and 2019. The volumes are as follows:

- *Discourses—Volume One: 2013–14: Living a Spiritually Rich Life*

- *Discourses—Volume Two: 2015: Re-Union of Soul and Spirit*

- *Discourses—Volume Three: 2016: A True New Birth*

- *Discourses—Volume Four: 2017: Gateway to the Infinite*

- *Discourses—Volume Five: 2018: Standing on the Threshold of Eternity*

- *Discourses—Volume Six: 2019: Writing in the Book of Life*

Regarding the use of images in this publication: Yogacharya David put great care, creativity, time, and intention into selecting images to complement his writings in each and every posting. When preparing his Discourses for publication, we found that certain images from unknown sources or those found to be under copyright could not be included. Every effort has been made to feature replacement images as close as possible to Yogacharya David's original selections. In a few instances where no similar substitute was available, a picture of Yogacharya David or a beloved saint has been offered instead.[1] Where we have placed substitute images is designated in the caption by a double asterisk **. For example: Yogacharya David at Anandashram, 2005.** Image attribution is in the Reference section at the end of this book.

OM TAT SAT AUM

---

[1]   Yogacharya David's original discourses can be found at www.crossandlotus.com

Introduction

Yogacharya David in Haridwar, India, 2005.

Dear Aspirant,

Whenever you begin a journey, you usually start with a destination in mind, a means of conveyance, and a map or landmarks to indicate that you are on the right path. Those of us following this path have God (Self) Realization as our Goal of goals. Our means of conveyance is God-remembrance, such as chanting God's Name, deepened meditation through Kriya Yoga, universal love and service, loving God, and discernment of Truth.

These writings often come in the early morning: a time when the day is quiet and fresh, an open page upon which to write. These thought-expressions come from an unfathomable Source, welling up from the quiet of the all-pervading Spirit. Reading these words has the power to lead you to the same Source from which they have flowed from within me.

The inspiration that fuels these writings comes to me with great power and clarity; however, mere words are incapable of holding all that is given. It is through inner attunement that the power in the words will lift you into the same Spirit that I experience in Super-consciousness, an uplifting power that is a passageway into realms divine.

Human words and thought are imperfect; it is only in pure Spirit that perfection is to be truly found. It is the purpose of these writings that we should rise together in the universal Spirit of God. Come, let us soar together and find truth and beauty unencumbered.

These discourses can act as markers upon your spiritual journey to make for safe and rapid progress. Unlike a scattered "hunt and peck" approach chosen by many taking them on "wild goose chases" only to become thoroughly lost, you will receive teachings of the purest quality that speed you on the most direct path to realization. Obstacles arise that create challenges for your journey—you can find inspiration here to help you meet those challenges.

These writings contain notes from pilgrimages and journeys that also (reader alert here!) have lessons upon the path embedded in them.[2]

With deepest love and blessings on your journey,
YOGACHARYA DAVID

---

2   Much of this Introduction comes from Yogacharya David's 2013–14 *Discourses, Volume One: Living a Spiritually Rich Life.*

DISCOURSES

January 3

GIVE LOVE

Give Love.**

I have been keenly aware of how much I have missed our coming together during these past months, when we were traveling and then with the current medical procedures.

One thing about love, it constantly wants to express itself. As I have often said, love is both a noun and a verb. First, it is like the sea, a state of Being content within its expansive Self. And second, love is like a flowing river, always moving and expressing itself. In realizing God, you simultaneously and easily have both aspects of love.

I remember the charming and instructive story of Papa; he had a cold and Mataji kept him wrapped up and gave instructions he was not to meet with devotees. Papa was pacing back and forth and finally said, "Sometimes Ramdas must do what he must do!" And he went out to talk with the devotees who sincerely desired to see him.

When I was going to meet with you all for our Christmas/New Year's Service, I too was lovingly warned not to do it; it was too soon after the operation. However, God within would not be denied. I started out the Service with a hoarse voice, but then later I was told that it grew to full strength as the talk proceeded. When God gives to you through this form, He also gives to me. I feel the river of love effortlessly flowing through me, and I too receive, even as it is given.

This is the great secret of love: the more we give, the more we receive. If, out of fear and resentment, we do not give, then we do not receive. This is never truer than in our relationships with husbands, wives, children, parents, or past best friends. It is true we can have our expectations dashed to the ground by others, especially those close to us. But, to choose to cut off the flow of love because of the pain and disappointment means that we sentence ourselves to a barren existence that dries up the very love we seek.

Courage means that we give love, even when it is not returned, that we even give love for hate, to love our enemy. This does not make us a "doormat" that can be stepped upon and be used by others, for this does neither them nor us any good. But, inwardly we do not close off our hearts even to those who have abused and betrayed our trust, for who needs love more than those who have closed hearts?

So let us pray for and love all of this world, just as it is. We see those who are filled with anger, hurt, and fear that seek to hurt others in retaliation. However, as an author said of Mahatma Gandhi's ahimsa philosophy, *An eye-for-eye and tooth-for-tooth would lead to a world of the blind and toothless.* All healing begins with love and wisdom, and healing ends with an immersion into love and wisdom. We may protect ourselves, but let us always be guided first by love, and not retaliate with anger, for anger perpetuates an endless cycle. Rather, wisely give love for anger for the resolution of your, and the world's, ills.

January 5

MASTER'S BIRTHDAY

Paramhansa Yogananda with his
book *Autobiography of a Yogi*, 1950.**

Today, we celebrate Master's (Paramhansa Yogananda's) birthday. What an absolute difference this great spiritual Master has made in my life, and in the lives of so many, many people. Certainly, the *Autobiography of a Yogi* continues to be a best seller and is a spiritual classic that has moved new generations to spiritual depths of feeling and perception that would have otherwise remained hidden.

It is difficult to measure the attainment of another; however, we can contrast Master's life and work to many who write books and more books and give public talks and never come close to being qualified to tie the latches of Master's shoes. Truly Master stands heads above so many others, with very few peers.

When Master drew Mother Hamilton to him, he set into motion a spiritually uplifting current that is transmitted to all of us. A disciple of Master's once told me that for any other person to be a guru after Master would "block his light." I had never heard such a load of ignorance in all my life (this would only be true if that one claiming to be a guru was filled with ego). I can tell you, and you do not need me to say it for you know it yourself, Mother's Light only added to Master's Light, making for a tremendous illumination for all.

There are many who are currently re-reading the *Autobiography of a Yogi*, others who are studying his lessons, and still others who are reading the books published in his name (although many of his books have been heavily edited, and in some cases, the "voice" of the author has nearly disappeared, still many of these sayings and writings are our only access, and the Master's Spirit will still inspire us in spite of the filters of heavy-handed editing). Master sought to make yoga and religion well-reasoned and understandable, demonstrable, and experiential by every man, woman, and child. Since seeking out happiness is a universal need, he showed that only by realizing God will you know lasting bliss and happiness. Therefore, the path to Self-realization is needed by everyone walking the globe.

My prayer is that with the marking of Master's birthday you will be inspired to delve deeper into his writings, and as the Master said, for every hour of reading, meditate for two hours. Your going deeper into God-consciousness is the greatest way to please the Master, then broadcast that Light of God you discover within yourself to the entire world. Just think of a world in which all people, everywhere, are striving to know the truth of God and to express His loving will in this world. This spiritual transformation is what the Master came to bring about, and each of us can do our part by following in his footsteps.

Master Paramhansa Yogananda—Happy Birthday—and thank you for being born and bringing this universal message of liberation and freedom to one and to all!

January 10

Work Is Love Made Visible

Yogacharya David, Mt Vernon, Washington, 2011.**

Activity is the natural outcome of static Spirit. Like the enormous lake that feeds the waterfall, that makes for the river that moves to the sea, so does transcendent Spirit, still and without end, naturally express itself as all creation and its creatures, including humankind.

Humankind is capable of the highest consciousness; however, as we see signs daily, it often times responds to its lowest nature. When we, as humans, put our minds upon attaining supreme God-consciousness, then the battle between our lowest and highest natures ensues. Lowest nature is selfish, greedy, and fearful, and it can be vicious. Highest nature is loving, kind, and full of service.

To attune ourselves to action based on the highest nature requires that we must be mindful of our thoughts, words, and actions. We know the difference when we are acting out of our highest nature and when we are responding to the demons within. All sincere aspirants will immediately self-correct when temporarily taken over by the seductive, devilish nature and re-align with angelic purity and Light.

> The great Kahlil Gibran declared that:
> Work is love made visible. And if you cannot work with love but only with distaste, it is better that you should leave your work . . . And what is it to work with love? It is to weave the cloth with threads drawn from your heart, even as if your beloved were to wear that cloth. It is to build a house with affection, even as if your beloved were to dwell in that house. It is to sow seeds with tenderness and reap the harvest with joy, even as if your beloved were to eat the fruit. It is to charge all things you fashion with a breath of your own spirit . . . [3]

To be in tune with loving activity, we first acknowledge that God is the Source of all movement, from subatomic electrons to vast galaxies, and everything in between. Let us not allow a mundane mindset to seep into our lives. Each moment is a unique expression of Spirit; there can be no such thing as "time to kill," for all time is filled with inexpressible Divine Feeling if we but have the eyes to see and the ears to hear.

First, make daily contact with God within through your deepening communion with the Infinite Spirit. Then mindfully enter

---

3   www.goodreads.com

into this world of activity by expressing joy, peace, and bliss, letting these qualities saturate your thoughts and words and guide your activities. All time and space are filled with sacred vibration, so live life fully and be an instrument of Spirit at all times and in all places.

January 17

Truth Makes You Free

Beloved Swami Ramdas.

The great Teachers of the world have given us the same truths. Buddha taught us to purify ourselves and have compassion for all creatures. Jesus Christ asked us to love all beings as we love ourselves. Krishna taught us to see the Divine in each and every one in the world. Mohammed taught us to submit to the will of God and be His instruments. If we but follow the teachings of these great Masters, we have no reason to quarrel among ourselves on any account.

—Swami Ramdas

There are those who like to point out the faults of religion as proof that there is no God. But it is an interesting thought experiment to think of this world without religion, no great religious leaders down through time who called struggling humankind to a higher life. Would this world really be better off?

For any honest appraisal you would have to know that the world is vastly improved for having Rama, Krishna, Lao Tzu, Buddha, Zoroaster, Jesus, and Muhammad, to name a few. The fact that we can find examples of hypocrites and abusers of faith has to be held in balance with the billions of souls who have striven for a better life because of their faith and spiritual practice.

All religious impulse ultimately leads to the singular goal of Self-realization. To see all of humankind in a march toward realization gives new meaning to world events. Through the struggle of sorting through the violence, ignorance, and darkness of collective consciousness, individual souls are inspired to rise above the tumultuous noise of this world to at last find transcendent Truth.

Realizing this Truth will alone free the soul from the thralldom of maya, universal ignorance. This world is rough play. However, when souls love one another, serve one another, and seek the Light within and in one another, this world consciousness is lifted higher, changed for the better, and this holds the promise of transforming this world into a peaceful garden, where the lion will lie down with the lamb.

Therefore, you should not be discouraged or doubtful when faced with the oppositional force you see in the world, and sometimes right within your own self. Rather, you should use these painful events as reminders that you are called to a higher life and to heed the call of those great God-men and God-women who have gone before you.

To realize this great Goal of humankind you must submit to the will of God and be His instrument, see the Divine in all creation and its creatures, and feel love and compassion for all. These practices purify your mind and will lead you to the blissful, universal vision in which faith and practice are supplanted by actual, realized experience. You then know the Truth, and that Truth sets you free.

Health Update: I continue to grow stronger each day. I have greater endurance and am in need of less rest. On Wednesday, I had an MRI of the brain and there was no sign of cancer. The surgeon called me his "star," and noted my recovery was very, very good—thanks to your many prayers and the miraculous power of the body to heal.

I am currently off all medication. I am taking food-grade dietary supplements of vitamins and minerals, and I have started a pro-biotic and pre-biotic regimen to reconstitute intestinal health after the antibiotics (that destroy good bacteria as well as the bad) and surgical assaults on the body.

I will see the oncologist on Monday and find out what he recommends for immunotherapy. There is a chance of cancerous cells being left in the stomach after the tumors have been removed. Since my immune system was more than capable of eliminating the melanoma on the skin—even without my notice—now, it is a matter of alerting the immune system to fight in the stomach as well. Thank you again for all your loving prayers; my rapid recovery is a clear demonstration of the power of prayer.

January 24

THE SIMPLE PEACE AND JOY IN FINDING GOD

Krishna as a Cowherd Boy, painting by
Gargi (Lakshmi), Anandashram, India.

One of the remarkable things about our spiritual path is that the benefit of its practice is not just for an imagined future, but it is realized in the here and now. Many who follow religious ideals think that the rewards for leading a spiritual life will not be known until arriving at a much-anticipated after-life. This deferred gratification can take many forms, but it justifies withholding from doing the things you would really like to do now, so that God and heaven may reward you later.

The spiritual "rewards" I have known have become embedded in my practice itself. Communing with God brings tremendous peace and bliss; being His instrument of service in the world gives me real joy and fulfillment, and living in complete surrender to Divine Will makes me know what right action truly is. I would not trade this life for any other.

The vows Mother had me take at Kriya have the same benefits. Not drinking alcohol or using recreational drugs was not easy in the beginning. But now it is not only easy, it makes me feel ill to even imagine going down that road. Not smoking cigarettes—how stupid would it be to take up that habit? And no sex without marriage—how much trouble, confusion, sorrow, and pain that saves me, and I would never know the more profound pleasures there are to be found in a committed, long-term marriage.

If I enact a thought experiment and imagine that there was no reward in an afterlife for living a life of truthfulness and spiritual discipline, would I regret having lived my life in this way? Absolutely not. The life I live here brings me the greatest happiness, and I would not change a single part of it.

There are many people who live lives they know are not in sync with their own highest good, yet they continue to do so without any serious thought to changing their habits. This lack of harmony with their inner knowing causes them great suffering. However, when your life comes into balance and you have congruity between Spirit, thought, word, and action, then you have a credible claim on peace today.

It can seem that others are zooming by you by taking shortcuts and living out of harmony with nature and Spirit's lawful principles. But believe me, they will never know the simple peace and joy you experience in finding God. Whether your dharma has you living in a cave or a mansion, whether you are in the humblest or most visible vocation, if it is right for you, then you need not envy anyone in this whole world, for you are exactly where your loving Creator has placed you. At times, it may be a great struggle to get there, but living in your true Self fulfills all of your heart's desires today, from moment to moment.

January 29

Decisions—Decisions—Decisions

Change Ahead.**

D ecision-making is a fascinating field of study. How we make decisions both large and small determines the kind and quality of life we live. Do you have one more bite to eat or push the plate away? Do you seek out new opportunities in life or do you stay in hiding? Do you strive for Self-realization or are you unconsciously and blindly stumbling through your days?

I have been in a transitional time these past few weeks. My recovery from a small intestine resection that removed three tumors has gone extremely well. As of today, I have no cancerous tumors as has been confirmed by a recent MRI of the brain and full-body CAT and PET scans: very happy news.

Now, I am faced with decisions about after-care; according to medical doctors, it is a very high likelihood that new tumors will grow. There are several allopathic drugs that may be partially or fully successful in keeping cancer from recurring, each with its unwanted side effects; I am also looking into a leading Naturopathic physician for supportive care as well as the ongoing treatment my marvelous chiropractic/neuro-link doctor provides. Each doctor gives his educated guess as to what the right course of action should be, plus I have had input from many of you on standard and alternative care as well.

How do I go about deciding what to do next? The first thing I do is go inside and commune with God. I still the mind, turn the whole matter over to Him. I feel peace and quiet in the inner Presence; that is my starting point. I know with certainty that God is in charge of this whole play. There is a mighty purpose behind all that He does, and I am content to play my role as He so chooses.

Being connected, I then gather information. What this and that doctor and care provider are saying, what friends and research tell me, assimilating all I can from external resources. I then take this accumulated knowledge and seek wisdom by mindfully surrendering all at the feet of God. "Oh Lord, here is the situation as You well know. What is the right thing for me to do at this time?" Then I open myself to His prompting. What do I feel right about doing in connection with Him? What thoughts come to me in that Light and with clarity? What brings me peace and a sense of "right action"?

Sometimes, the message is to simply rest in Him. When the time is right, some thought, a sense of direction, comes out of the peaceful silence that makes me know what to do next. Over the years, this process of decision-making has never failed me. I can directly compare it to times when I have not used this process; it correlates closely with making bad decisions when I ignored God.

We expend an amazing amount of energy taking false steps and burn up in anxious energy, all to no avail. A favorite image comes from the blacksmith. He heats the metal to the right temperature before he shapes and bends the metal to good effect. The blacksmith knows he can pound away forever if the metal is not hot enough and he will get nowhere. When the metal is ready, a few well-placed blows may be all that is needed.

Even so, God may have us in the fires of purification; we desperately would like to jump out of those flames! However, by staying still and centered throughout it all, we take His cue as to when the hammer blows should come in order to bring it about correctly. This all-important timing is critical to fulfilling His will.

If, in your silence, you have no answer, that is a red light. You may get a yellow light to proceed with caution, or the green light comes for an all-out go! This knowingness requires your trust and your willingness to be still before you act. Decision-making like this becomes clear from practice and patience. When you get the knack of it, it will be very obvious to you when it is Divine Will that is operating through you and when you are being governed by the dictator-ego.

As you can easily apprehend, decision-making is a fascinating field of study, and when you take the time and make the effort to go deeper, it brings you into harmony with your true Self and with God. In this way, the world you live in is a great teacher, and the large and small challenges you face provide the very means to achieve the greatest goal in life, your oneness with God.

Health Note: As mentioned above, I have completed a series of tests: an MRI of the brain, and CAT and PET scans of the rest of the body. There are no signs of any tumors in this body. Blood tests and all other metrics have come back positive. This is all great news! Now, the focus is on keeping this body in perfect health. There are several options on the table, and it will be interesting to see what God decides. All is in His keeping. Jai Gurus, Victory to God!

February 2

MOTHER'S SILVER ANNIVERSARY

Mother's Silver Anniversary Card.

W hat a joy it has been to mark the Silver Anniversary of Mother Hamilton's Mahasamadhi. As the saying goes, *Many hands make light work.* Larry designed a card to mark the occasion; Jill created a beautiful cake for the potluck, along with all the devotees whose loving contributions made for a delicious lunch after service.

However, what stands out most for me from the day is the feeling of Mother's presence, her thoughts and her love pervading the Service and the day. I had the thought that I should say something about Mother's place in history and her role in the evolution of world-consciousness, but at the moment, that seems distant compared to her loving, intimate divine presence—the cherished merging of Guru and disciple.

It often happens that when giving a spiritual talk, I am keenly aware of Mother's thoughts and spiritual power in close connection to my own. That presence has all the hallmarks of God's Presence, only it has the unmistakable print of Mother's personality and consciousness upon it. It is a most remarkable communion with Mother that manifests all the purity, wisdom, and power of unalloyed God-consciousness.

And this is part and parcel of Mother's teachings and life example: you must strive to overcome ego in order to know God, and when that is accomplished, then it is God who manifests as the Divine Ego. This is described in the Mystical Crucifixion when Jesus gives up the ghost (the ego) and returns with the power of the Holy Ghost (or the Divine Ego).

The Divine Ego is enabled to manifest all the attributes of God; for then, in truth, it may be said, "I and Thou are one." This great event is a tremendous boon to the world, for it brings all the purity of God into this physical realm in ways that are unique. Mother was, and is, just such a blessing for this world.

For all those who recognize the truth of Mother's existence, a deep and personal blessing is theirs. Through inner attunement, Mother's love, wisdom, and power are available. Just as a radio can receive messages from invisible signals, and a transmitter can broadcast the same, so built within a human being a soul may receive and broadcast spiritual consciousness.

The source of that power may come from a spiritually charged place on earth such as an ashram or a holy site; it can also be derived from making a connection with an embodied or transcendent spiritual Being, or directly from the Source-Being of God. An attuned receiver may in turn become a transmitter, sending out those blessings to all the earth. It is a fact that we all have that capacity; only at this time, most individuals are filled with radio-static of worldly concerns and attachments.

By going deep into meditation, setting aside all limitations, and knowing God, you may be just such a receiver/transmitter. All the wisdom of God, all the love, joy, and bliss may be yours, and you may in turn give that same Spirit to one and to all. There would be nothing more pleasing to Mother or any of the great spiritual masters this world has ever known than for you to follow in their footsteps and become what they became, for there is no limit to God's power, love, and wisdom.

The more joy you manifest the more joy Mother feels for you; this adds to her already superabundant joy! So let us honor Mother's life and teachings today and everyday by being all that we are meant to be in Divine Consciousness, until we merge our little selves with the universal Divine Being, God, even as Mother did.

Reverend Jill's cake offering to Mother topped with rose petals.

February 7

THE SWORD IS IN KRISHNA'S HAND

Krishna dancing on the head of
the poisonous snake, Kaliya.**

The internal journey of a life is where life is really lived, for it is the creator of all activities. It may come as a surprise to many how much of an internal life we have, even as infants and small children. In fact, it is only through conditioning that mental reflection is sometimes blocked out presenting us with a life that is simply reactive to the conditions of this world.

It is in the practice of meditation that we come up against how conditioned we are by this world. Even when we are in a safe meditation place, the mind races with preoccupations: "What happened yesterday? What will happen today? A careful recall of things that happened years ago (or lifetimes ago). What will happen years from now?" All these thoughts can fill our mind when our whole intention is meant to become still in the here and now.

In these past weeks, I have been absorbing what doctors have been telling me, what different books and people are saying, taking it all in and digesting it for possible future action. In addition, I have been a witness to how this mind and body are reacting to all of this information.

When I focus on the condition of the body in the here and now, I feel fine. I know that it can take some months for the anemia to completely right itself, but I can walk up hills and run on my rebounder each day with a building endurance that replicates times of past good health. My incision is healing very nicely and there are no tumors. Life is good.

In the midst of all of this is what doctors tell me is a looming problem, what the oncologist called the sword of Damocles. Now, in the story, the sword of Damocles is held by a hair and hangs over the head of the king; it may give way at any moment. The other day, I was running on the rebounder, listening to a song about Krishna and looking at a beautiful picture I have of Master. Suddenly, a mental image came to me of the sword of Damocles above me, and instead of hanging by a hair, it was held by smiling Krishna. How lovely is that?

The reality is that facts are not always truth. The fact is there is a statistical probability of new tumors growing. The truth is no one knows for sure. Another truth is that the mind is a powerful player in health: hope, faith, love, and trust all enhance the health of the body. Also, there are the healthy habits of eating and exercise that help create an inhospitable bodily atmosphere (what one researcher calls the "terrain") for cancer cells.

So, first of all, I choose God (smiling Krishna is in charge of the sword); I choose the empowerment of choice for healthy habits;

I choose love, and I choose to continue to learn, grow, serve, and to be happy!

There are many examples of people who live long lives, unfulfilled and unhappy. There are other examples of those who had shorter lives but were quite the opposite; in fact, they changed the world in infinitely better ways. The lives of Jesus, Adi Shankaracharya, St. Francis, Swami Rama Tirtha, the "Little Flower" St. Teresa, and Swami Vivekananda may have been short, but oh what lives they lived!

The sword is in Krishna's hand, and while I am here, I will sing, and dance, and serve, and be in the joy of God for all the days of my life. And who knows, God may not be done with me yet!

February 13

QUIET DETERMINATION

Amazing tenacity for life: Tree in Bryce Canyon, Utah.**

A devotee was telling me about her sister who had had cancer. After her treatment was over, the staff wanted to leave her port in, just in case the cancer returned, and they would need its use again. The sister said absolutely not, the cancer was not going to come back!

She then turned to me and said, "I have not heard that kind of statement from you." I told her that I had that as a mental attitude, but God had not confirmed that there would be no new cancerous growths. However, her statement has made me consider the subject of making a bold declaration that the cancer will not return.

I thought about my mindset, the way I have felt guided in making decisions about treatment, and ways to focus my mind. I made note that my whole orientation has been to remove the tumors, and now that that is done, to research, inwardly and outwardly, into what I can do to keep this body tumor-free.

I have not had a port, nor has there been an occasion that required me to make a bold decision that would proclaim an absolute faith in being cancer-free into the future. So, what do I say?

As I thought this over, I came to realize that my attitude, and how I have felt guided by Divine Will, is a quiet determination to remain cancer-free. Tumors do not belong in this body; they are destructive to this body, and I reject their presence!

One of my mantras has been, "I have a clear mind (memory and concentration were affected by the anemia), I have clear vision (also affected by the anemia), and I have a clear abdominal cavity (past location of tumors)." My memory, concentration, and vision have all vastly improved and the tumors are gone. When I say the word "clear," I experience Light and life-force sweeping through, making all clean, clear, and operating at its highest caliber.

Since childhood, I have had the sense that my life would really begin when I turned fifty, and I would live until my eighties. It is true that my life took on new dimensions that made me live in a completely new way when I started my sixth decade, and it continues to resonate that living into my eighties seems right.

It is not in my nature to make bold proclamations, but this quiet determination has been more of my style in life and continues to be so now. There is no part of me that feels that life is over; I will love astonishing my oncologist by having a long life! Without a hint of defeatism, I am at peace, surrendering the results to God.

For many people, surrender means defeat, but not for the devotee of God. For the devotee, surrender means being in the loving care of a most beneficent God who will see to it that every part of life is fulfilled for the highest good of all. I stand in that Light and rejoice over the opportunity to live life to its fullest, to be His servant every moment of every day, and surrender my life at His sacred feet.

Post Note: I do hope you are not tired of reading about my journey to perfect health. I do not see it as my journey alone, but that this is a description of all journeys in life, encapsulated in the clothing of this narrative. The choice of attitude we face life's challenges with is what is common to all of us. I have heard from many of you that you have valued my descriptions and have received benefit from them. I will only say that my intention is not to focus undue attention upon this body, but to see it as a paradigm for inner attunement to the one living God and the spiritual masters we have been blessed by who have walked this earth.

P.P.S. Carla and I leave for Boulder City, Nevada early Sunday morning, where we will once again begin our southern pilgrimage. We will return on March 15, in time for the first immunotherapy vaccine injection and for an Easter celebration here on Camano Island.

February 18

LIVING IN THE PRESENT

Lake Mead from campsite the morning after the storm.

We have returned to our pilgrimage south and rejoined our "Heaven on Wheels" tour of North America. I do not consider it a break from our pilgrimage that we should have returned to Camano Island for surgery and treatment, only that the pilgrimage has taken us on twists and turns not anticipated.

Thanks to Rick and Judy, our RV was in excellent shape on our return to Lake Mead campground. We were, in fact, just parked feet away from where we had last left it, only in a fenced storage area, and now we are camped next door at Boulder Beach, overlooking Lake Mead.

It is interesting how the mind processes the past in the here and now. It is as if the surgery, just 10 weeks ago today, and the subsequent recovery were but a dream. When at Anandashram, we sat with Swami Satchidananda, facing a cultivated field sitting on concrete seats made for our daily visits. Swamiji led us in the song, "Row, row, row your boats, gently down the stream. Merrily, merrily, merrily, merrily, life is but a dream." Those were sweet moments, and when taken deep within, this song is very meaningful.

Our higher human brain functions mean that we can ruminate more on the past and spend more time anticipating the future. While these functions enable us more far-ranging thought, they can come at a price as well. Past experiences, especially traumas, can loop in the brain like a film played over and over, creating new feelings of distress every time it plays, as if it is all happening again. Our anticipation of the future can take an obsessive turn in which we think of what is to come; when it is a happy thought, we are happy, but when they are troublesome thoughts, we become very anxious.

This focus on the past and the future can absolutely rob us of the present. God-experience occurs only in the present; it also heals us from past trauma—anticipate being wrapped in the Divine Presence, always. God-experience places both future and past into their right perspective and gives us the great joy of living in the present.

There are some who never find joy in living in the present. Instead, they heap on loads of trouble borrowed from the past, and imagined anxiety from the future, feeling that life is an unbearable burden. Is there no place, then, for anticipating what life may bring? Of course, we benefit from preparing for what may come. However, there is a huge distance between living in constant angst and responding to a concern for what is coming.

Last night, a storm came through. In anticipation, we placed outdoor chairs under cover and did all we could to prepare for wind and rain. That preparation was done in the here and now, and while preparing, we sang the Name of God (or we could have sung, "Row, row, row your boat!"), feeling joy in the activity. And when the storm came, we felt we were wrapped in the warm protection of the Divine Presence. Then when cleaning up after the storm this early morning, I also sang God's Name, feeling joy in doing what needed to be done.

As Jesus of Nazareth asked, can you grow taller by anxious thought? We may need a shot of adrenaline now and then to accomplish some task, but constant anxiety is such an awful waste. Let us learn to have God-experience here, now. Watch how the here-and-now God-experience lends a halo of peace and joy to both the past and the future. In this way, the omnipresence of the Infinite glows from every nook and cranny of our mind and life-experience. Now, peace, love, and joy are our constant and abiding companions through every moment of every day for our pilgrimage through life!

February 21

OVERCOMING FEAR AND ANGER

Boondocking in the desert.

There are tests that come to all people regardless of their belief system or spiritual development. Highly realized souls can take on the world's "sins" (errors) in ways that others cannot, due to their identification with God. Some imagine that realizing God will be the end of all challenges; however, God has become everything there is, and therefore, there is nothing outside of His purview or that of His beloved one's.

When you are in intimate connection with God, how can you not also know His creation: the good, the bad, and the ugly? The difference for the realized master is the certain knowledge that God is his, and he is God's. Normally, souls become deluded when they meet the bad or the ugly. In this delusion, there is felt to be a vast separation between the soul, the world, and God.

Recently, I came up against a case of murderous anger in a soul; in reality, this anger stemmed from a deep fear. In self-absorption, this individual felt the world was not meeting certain needs. Such anger and fear are not uncommon, but how sad it is when they result in a looping dialogue for which there is no solution. It is because fear and anger are emotionally charged and self-sustaining; if there is a change in one area of dissatisfaction in life, then another will crop up that will be found to be equally dissatisfying. Thus, fear and anger lead to a never-ending cycle. This person's anger clung to me like cigarette smoke permeates clothes and hair and everything it touches.

The real solution is to realize the Divine Intention behind all the world's activities, even the bad and ugly. With this solution alone, a peace that surpasses all understanding comes into the heart and soul—a peace unshakable. Without this solution, fear and anger will corrupt the soul, making it ugly and distorted beyond the recognition of its original design by the Creator.

This solution of knowing God must come to every soul, and it begins with genuine surrender and humility. A heartfelt prayer must ask for Divine intervention to let go of all fear and anger. Then, with one's whole thought, feeling, and will, he or she must align individual will with Divine Will.

As I witnessed firsthand with both Mother Hamilton and Swami Satchidananda, a spiritual life is not hiding from the difficult parts of life and all of its complexities; rather, it is often putting yourself right into the middle of it. The difference is that you have now placed yourself on God's side; there is no separation, and that makes all the difference. As I placed this individual's anger at the feet of God, lit some incense, and gave it all to Him, the residue left me, leaving only peace and compassion.

If you have not yet realized God fully, it means you are harboring fear and/or anger that does not allow you to experience this surpassingly beautiful peace. Expose your innermost workings before God, surrender all that you knowingly or unknowingly are keeping for yourself, then lay it all at the feet of your infinite Beloved. Experience His peace as never before, then you will go on to be a Light unto this world.

Health Update: All is going along very well in our continued pilgrimage; we are in a beautiful desert on the border of Joshua Tree National Park's south entrance. Rick and Judy are our close neighbors; we are boondocking on Bureau of Land Management (BLM) land under a full moon and magnificent star-scape.

The question came to me early this morning, "How do I create a mental image to direct my body on a cellular level, and continue to be tumor-free?" I have had a generalized thought of Light flowing into the affected area, but that did not seem to be sufficiently powerful; I knew I needed something more specific.

I thought of white blood cells, the body's combat-ready soldiers, cordoning off and destroying the microscopic cells that do not belong. Even more powerful are the "special unit" soldiers, "take no prisoner" combatants, the battle-hardened killer T cells. Killer T cells can drill holes into the seemingly impervious cancer cells, and with repeated penetration, the cancer cells collapse and die. Visualizing these white and killer T cells surrounding and killing cancer cells and prohibiting them from migrating elsewhere has given my mind a useful and powerful focus. I see these soldiers of the immune system filled with an inner Light of Divine power and energy fighting the cells that do not belong! Yes, that will do nicely.

P.S. Please keep X in your prayers. This last week, it was confirmed that she has a cancerous tumor in her colon. The medical opinion at this time is that the surgical removal of the tumor may be all that is needed at this point; more will be known after the procedure. May all souls strive for, and attain, perfect health in body, mind, and spirit!

February 26

BIRTHDAY GREETINGS

Climbing on Ladders Trail, Painted
Canyon, Southern California.

Being it is my birthday, I have been put into a mood of remembrance. My first memory of the life of this body begins with being in the womb of my mother. I remember the sounds of her heartbeat, the comfort of the womb. I was also aware of who I was as a soul. I had foreknowledge of aspects of my life to come, and recent memories of what my life was before coming into this body. I knew that this life would be difficult compared to the life I had before, and I had some trepidation about it.

Other memories come in. The difficulties I anticipated were of a more psychological and spiritual nature, for my physical needs were taken care of, though I found being in the physical body a challenge compared to the light body I had before. I had a loving mother and a dutiful father, and two older brothers who seemed to live in a different world, being just that much older than I.

I remember our family's first television and when a "play date" consisted of our mother throwing us out of the house and telling us not to come back in until lunch. Tether ball games at the neighbors', basketball in the driveway, playing catch by the hour, imagining being Yogi Berra or Roger Maris of my favorite New York Yankees. There was the excitement of the first color television and Walt Disney's "Wonderful World of Color," and watching the Beatles for the first time on Ed Sullivan's "Really Big Shew." Imagination turned the whole house into a flying saucer and made me a general of armies with strategies to plan. Getting up early to watch rockets take off from Cape Canaveral, then almost withheld breath as I watched the first steps taken on the moon.

Then, there was my first car, a jeep inherited from my older brother, then in the Marines. Playing baseball, football, and wrestling were major themes; unfortunately, academics were ignored (one teacher commented that I did more work trying to get out of doing schoolwork than if I just did it, and I rejoined that was true but it was more fun this way)! What could he do? Not until college and I was paying for my education did I take it seriously and have to make up for all of those lessons I had not learned earlier!

The first time I "fell in love" took me into a new world. The breakup of that love took me into another new world that had been germinating all my life, a spiritual awakening. It was not my second birth, but it was the dedicated gestation period to being born again that would take many years to accomplish. Learning to drive a semi-truck, moving to the west side of the mountains, working for a year or so, then going to one more year of college as I could afford it, traveling to Europe and Africa, and of course meeting Mother Hamilton, which stands above all other life-experiences.

It is amazing now to slide in review over so many years, consolidating so many experiences. Life takes on an entirely new view when seen from the rear-view mirror, smoothing out bumps, soothing wounds, and clarifying lessons. What seemed an eternity of time then, seems only a blip on the screen now: remembered but pacified. One other thing, all these experiences are now placed in a context of meaning that was oftentimes absent at the time. I see the great adventure of this life as refining and purifying consciousness, to make it ready for a true New Birth.

And this is the great lesson for me, from the time I was in my mother's womb until today—the meaning of life is found in the evolution of consciousness and its ultimate merging with Divine Consciousness.

It is finding union with the Divine that places all life-experience into its proper role. All life serves one ultimate, glorious purpose that makes it all worthwhile. And that is what is monumentally clear to me as I turn 62.

February 28

BEST BIRTHDAY PRESENT

Nature's Living Cathedral, Palm Canyon, California.

Wordlessly, a command came to all four in our wandering group: *Sit here and meditate.* Rick, Judy, Carla, and I all find repose in a copse of California fan palm trees, a cool respite from a warm, sun-baked day. I am spontaneously drawn within—the body and surroundings fade from consciousness as peace envelops my receptive soul.

This place, Palm Canyon, had been a Native American habitat for many hundreds, perhaps thousands, of years, an oasis in the midst of a harsh desert environment. There are places in nature that have pure, powerful, uplifting currents systemic to their nature. Other places have been the haunts of saints and realized beings that take on their vibration, and that feeling remains. Then there are places that are a combination of both, natural temples that are supported by holy men and women who find it conducive to be in a salubrious environment, and make it even more so through their own uplifted states of minds.

An Agua Caliente Cahuilla (Kaw-we-ah) woman had talked about picking up a stone, and the thought that one of her ancestors could have picked up that same stone hundreds of years ago denoted to her an unbroken continuity of time and spirit. To have such a feeling for a place, connecting you with tribe, ancestors, and unity of spirit, is a long step towards experiencing the unifying Spirit that ties individual consciousness to the Supreme Consciousness of Omnipresence and Omniscience.

The wind is now whispering to us as it blows through the fan palm leaves. We are caressed and held in the sacred feeling of this place. Mother Hamilton came right here in 1958 and also experienced its extraordinary nature. Thus, even as the Cahuilla woman felt her commonality with ancestors when picking up a rock, we experience it too in Mother's spirit seeping into the peace and tranquility we feel, spanning the decades and making us feel her near. While God is known to be equally present everywhere in His creation, He seems to be more "equally present" in some places than others!

In contrast to this uplifting vibrancy, there are definitely places that hold a negative, dark, even evil, vibration as well. One day, I took a walk in a park that had been a monastery. An outdoor temple was carved in a nook. As I approached the rustic altar available to the public, I felt a dark, evil wall of energy. Definite thought impressions: this altar had been used earlier for black magic ceremonies, and its residue left an ugly aura behind: immature souls looking to bolster sagging egos.

And now, what a blessing it is to be here, in this sacred place, giving and receiving holy breath, a living cathedral. As we evolve as a race of humankind, it is ennobling to think of raising this planet's consciousness into the highest realms of Spirit: a heaven in, and on, earth. We begin with our homes, then the places we go, both in nature and in the busy marts of humans. However, for me, today, there is no better birthday present than to be here in this place of pilgrimage, with Mother, and now with all of you, in this home of deepest shanti-peace.

March 2

HONORING THIS AMAZING TEMPLE

Birthday cake made by Judy based on a recipe from Master's kitchen.[4]

C arla and I attended a nutrition class at the hospital and a nutritionist came to my room to talk to me about supporting this body in recovery. I have also been reading about ways to help the body maintain optimum health. There are some takeaway lessons that I think everyone can benefit from.

Of course, it is good when you have a pithy saying that sticks with you and actually leads to a positive change of behavior. One of these was from the nutritionist. She said that most people only chew their food just enough to keep themselves from choking to

---

4   Birthday cake made by Judy based on a recipe from Master, adapted and described by Angela in the Cross and Lotus Journal, "From the Master's Kitchen." We substituted grapeseed oil and used 70 percent chocolate. It was delicious.

death! That is quite an image. The fact is that an important part of digestion occurs from mastication (chewing) and the mixing of saliva with the food.

Some years ago, I started to discipline myself to chew completely what I had in my mouth and swallow before taking another bite. I actually laid my fork down between bites to support my doing this. I was amazed at how difficult this was in the beginning. I was used to taking another load full of food before I had chewed and swallowed the previous mouthful. Amazing! I found several benefits from eating this way: I enjoyed the flavor of food and noticed subtleties as never before; it slowed my eating and improved digestion, and I was more tuned into when I was actually full and therefore could choose to stop eating, even if I had more food on my plate.

In the class, the nutritionist made a point: eat food that looks like it comes from a farm. "You do not see Pop-Tarts growing on stalks in the fields," she said. Eat whole-grained foods; eat foods that you can recognize from the farm, not overly processed foods that add loads of sugar and unpronounceable ingredients (if you cannot pronounce it, you probably should not be eating it).

There are a lot of foods that have specific effects on the body: some fight free radicals that can cause cancer, some are anti-inflammatory, and so on. However, simply eating more fruits and a rainbow color of vegetables (fresh or frozen) would cover a lot of healthy territory. One source said that if you eliminate fries, potato chips, and the lettuce and tomato from a hamburger, over 50 percent of Americans would not even have one serving (usually a half-cup or a cup) of vegetables and fruit a day. Isn't that astounding? Not even one serving! Remember, food is not only the fuel your body needs, but it is also the original pharmacy for healing and keeping your body well.

It is amazing how much abuse this body can take. Perhaps that is not always to our benefit, because we start to think it doesn't make any difference how we treat it. However, unhealthy patterns tend to have a cumulative effect and when our body gives us trouble, we feel betrayed; the real betrayal usually occurred many years before, based on how we fed and treated the body.

No discussion on natural health can be complete without mentioning exercise—a vital component. Getting up from your chair and going for a good walk every day would be a huge step in the right direction for most people. Practice the yoga postures Briana describes so well; I have asked her to adapt some of the poses so that you can do them at your desk, and she has started this in the most recent Cross and Lotus Journal. You will find you will feel better, have more energy, and sleep better, plus if you can walk in a nice environment, you will enjoy yourself immensely; chanting is a wonderful occupation for the mind while you walk. Think of Papa walking from one end of India to the other!

I know that none of these principles are new to you. However, as I said in the beginning, if something sticks with you and actually changes your behavior, then it will truly have value. Perhaps reading these words will get you refocused so that you can really treat your body as the magnificent bio-organism it is. Chew your food thoroughly, eat foods that look like they come from a farm, and go for a good walk every day.

When you investigate the marvelous ways in which the body has been constructed—I mean truly amazing intelligence that has gone into its design—and then how little thought you give to feeding it high-quality fuel and providing what it needs for optimum living, it is really the height of ingratitude that you show your Creator for the miraculous gift He has bestowed upon you, if you are not doing so now. If not, then it is high time to show that appreciation, starting today, by living with healthy habits and honoring this amazing Temple.

March 6

DESERT PURITY

Our current "backyard."

The desert has been the haunt of God-seeking souls since earliest recorded history. Certainly, there is room for seclusion in the desert; few others wish for the extremes that it brings: from hot to cold. From a distance, it is seemingly lifeless and barren, but when close up, it displays an amazing amount and variety of life-forms. Truly, the desert is a place of extremes.

However, extremes and even lonely existence do not completely explain why aspirants have sought out the desert's refuge. The reason is clear enough when you are in its midst: the desert has purity. Even though it has dust on the ground, the air is pure, the vibration is clean, and there is room to think and to be. While such purity is not unique to the desert, still it has it in abundance.

We are currently boondocking on BLM (Bureau of Land Management) land near Wickenburg Arizona; that means that we have traveled on rustic roads to slightly prepared camp spots, oftentimes spread out so that we can see our neighbors in a distance or not at all; all for no cost. We have to be self-contained, that is have our own water, bathroom, holding tanks, etc. Generally, there is no one around to regulate things; we are expected to be on good behavior and treat the land well.

Participating in these lonely retreats is a large part of what I anticipated when starting this pilgrimage: this feeling of purity, the air, the expanded space, the quiet vibration, and even the desert's beauty. I grew up in the desert, but it was not particularly beautiful. Here, the rock formations and the surprising variety of cactus makes the landscape interestingly beautiful.

The birds calling with complex songs, five cows passing by (making Carla think of India), little rabbits scampering, and soaring hawks above all make up our neighbors. But most of all, it is the expansiveness and purity of Mother Nature that makes my soul merge with Spirit in a timeless and effortless fashion.

Saint Anthony lived his adult years as a monk and recluse in the desert of Egypt, living to be 105. He came to peace with himself after encountering the demons he found lurking in the darkness of ancient burial caves. Anthony had been born to wealth (in the 3rd century A.D.), but one day he heard Christ's teachings to sell all you have and give it to the poor; he took the words literally and did just that, after providing for his sister since their parents had both died. When, as an old man, he walked out of the desert and onto the bustling streets of Alexandria, he may as well have been Jesus come again for all the stir he made. Anthony, in his simpleness and reclusiveness, had a major influence upon early Christianity.

While we have the luxury of a modern RV, unthought of by brave Anthony, we too are able to enjoy this desert retreat. The stars emblazon the nightly sky, Orion's Belt and the Big Dipper adorn their respective quadrants, and the resounding Om–Amen attunes the mind to infinite Spirit. A vibrational quiet insulates the receptive soul from the constant restlessness of modern life.

One of those opposites of the desert: it is in silent reclusiveness that my consciousness effortlessly merges into all-consciousness, and through that to you. For, in touching the fabric of God, one must be connected to all that God is, including His creation.

Ram's Fun: going for a hike we walked by Mark's RV, a beautifully painted pickup and compact horse trailer; the trailer has been converted by this cabinet maker into a home for himself and his two dogs. One of several signs tastefully painted on his trailer said yeti. Since we are in a Bigfoot RV, I ask him if he has seen any yetis today (yeti being the Bigfoot of the Himalayas). He says not today, but he goes on to explain Yeti coolers are a sponsor for his trip; the coolers, he tells us, sell from four hundred to three thousand dollars! He assures us that on two occasions the coolers have saved his life during his travels. Once when the temperatures soared to 140 degrees and the cooler kept ice cold for a week, and once when the temperatures dropped to nine degrees and it kept his food from freezing.

He says that he is writing a book about the horse's influence on the West. He had planned to write the book in four years while he traveled exclusively in his horse trailer, but since that time was now up, he realized that he needed two more years to complete it. Mark contracts for cabinet work along the way to pay his expenses: "I earn my way!" He had been recently photographing wild mustangs and a wild burro. For the finale of his book and his six years of travel, he plans on living for a year with a horse, and his two dogs, in his trailer; in fact, he has the horse already lined up for the privilege! Ram has no end of fun entertaining us with His "special edition" manifestations.

March 10

IMPOSSIBLE TASKS

The tiny white dot is our RV in expansive Mother Nature.

Impossible tasks seem to be ahead of me, things to be accomplished before I am to leave this body. However, what seems to be impossible to me is easily accomplished by an all-powerful God.

When I survey what needs to be done, it looks to be an unconquerable mountain. But that is just me, my localized view. I would be a fool to rely on my own resources as a human being.

God one time gave me an apt simile: He made me think of when I first had a computer, a Commodore 64, more of a plaything compared to a full-scale personal computer of today. Later, when I had moved up to a larger scale computer, Larry talked me into accessing something called the internet. I was not sure how that would be useful to me at the time. I will remind you this was the early 1990s and in order to access the internet you had to dial it up. If you were fortunate, it gave all the appropriate beep and bop noises that made you know you had made the connection, then you had to type in the exact address filled with backslashes and dots in order to go to a specific internet address. I finally gave it a try and moved into a much larger computing world.

A while later, a close friend needed a pharmaceutical drug that was available in England but not here. Amazingly, I was able to order it for her and a great positive result came about. Of course, the internet has evolved in leaps and bounds since then and billions of people could not imagine their lives without it today. In a similar way, we hear about the inner-net, our connection with God. It can seem distant and perhaps non-relevant, something more for those "church-going-folks" than something really practical, even essential.

We simply don't see it, and as a result, we miss the greatest, most powerful tool available to us in life—in a similar way that I did not see how my little computer would one day be connected to the collective computing power of servers and data banks from around the world through the internet. The inner-net also evolves; the more we use it, the more connected we become. What seems perhaps cumbersome in the beginning, the occasional "hits" we get through meditation and prayer, becomes more refined, smoother, and wide-ranging as we make the connection again and again.

I know that the tasks I have to do in the world are really God's tasks. He has demonstrated in this past year that this body is not to be here forever, and the question naturally comes: will I be able to do all that He has given me to do? This is an important question. But if I am insulated in my humanness, the answer is intimidating. When I open myself to the inner-net, the answer is illuminating. This is God's Work. I am but a cog in His machine, and if He finds this cog unusable, He will toss it aside and find another that meets His needs!

Is this a cold and unnerving answer? No, it is actually a relief. While it is my part to strive to accomplish all that He has given me, and believe me it is of the utmost importance to me that I do so, still, it is according to His will. Through his Omnipotence, Omniscience, and Omnipresence, He will accomplish all that He has set out to do; of that, there is no doubt. My part is to willingly, full-heartedly, and mindfully live each day as His instrument. That is all I can do, that is what He needs from me, and He will see to the rest.

Already I have new helpers who are working daily to do part of what He has set out for me to do. In this, I can take perfect repose; it is unfolding according to His will. I am to remain connected to the all-important inner-net: the power and intelligence of Divine Consciousness. With this connection streams His peace, joy, and direction. There is nothing more that I want or need. So, for what God has given me to do, for what He has given you to do, Victory to God! Victory to the Light! For all sentient beings, everywhere!

March 12

A TEST OF LOVE

A Beautiful Desert Bloom: Today Is, and Tomorrow Is Gone.

Two days ago, God put me through a most interesting test, for what purpose only He knows. I was residing in Him when He lifted me up and put me into a very specific state of mind. In this state, He asked me, "If you have no afterlife when you die, will you still live the life you do?"

My mind went to the very powerful and intimate experiences God has given me in knowing my past lives, my life beyond this body, my eternal Self. For the purposes of this test, God put all those experiences at a great distance; a veil dropped down in my consciousness that made this profound awareness null and void. I knew this is what He wanted, so I accepted this limitation.

So, I asked God, "My experience of You in this life remains the same. You are as immediate, intimate, intelligent, loving, and blissful as You ever have been, only there is no afterlife for me?"

"Yes."

"And You are eternal, You will carry the memory of me, but I will cease to exist other than that memory?"

"Yes."

I was made to see death as a final curtain in which all individual awareness ceased; I no longer existed. Then I thought of living my life now, with this immediate awareness of God within me, the very source of my Being, an intimate intelligence weaving itself effortlessly through my thoughts, the loving Presence as my constant Beloved, the peace and bliss He gives me: all of that remains the same. Only, in the end, it is the end for me, nothing more. Would I regret or change my mode of living, being, having God as my all and all?

The thought that came to me is that I would be a fool not to have God with me, right up until my last breath. I went with the thought experiment that felt real in the moment, and that God was obviously orchestrating. I reflected on the paradox that I would remain in God's consciousness, that He is eternal, therefore I am eternal, however, although He remembered me, my "I" awareness was gone. I accepted this condition. And given this condition, I would in no way live my life differently; I would never wish that He was not part and parcel of my existence, moment to moment, until that final end. Of this, I was absolutely certain. And with this answer, I felt an indescribable freedom come over me.

After some little time, the same paradoxical thought came back to me, "If I exist in God's awareness eternally, then I am eternal, even if I cease to exist," and in that thought, God removed the veil He had placed in my mind and He laughed, like a child playing a game. It was obvious that in Him I am eternal; we all are; we can be nothing else.

I remember reading about an early Jewish sect, the Sadducees, who believed in God, and lived according to His law, but they did not believe in an afterlife because it was never mentioned in the Torah. Their virtue of living according to God's law was that their adherence to that life, the goodness of it, was passed down for ten generations; they lived according to the law for their children and their children's children. It struck me as strange that these people believed in God but had no thought of an afterlife.

But God's test for me was even different from that, for He gave me no thought that in living the life I do, I would have any good effect down the line for anyone else; there was nothing at the end, just the finality of nothingness. And my love for Him was absolutely the same. I would, and do, want nothing else but Him. He is the best of life in everything I see, touch, taste, smell, hear, think, and do—He is the cream of existence in everything that is. It is truly sufficient to have Him here, and now. And with that thought in my mind, He laughs at the game He has played; an eternal joy rolls and rolls throughout all creation!

March 20

FOLLOWING IN THE FOOTSTEPS
OF THE GREAT ONES

Christ in Gethsemane, painting by
Heinrich Hofmann, c. 1890.**

There are layers to the brain that we can trace from the most primitive to the most sophisticated. The amygdala in the limbic system is involved with instinctual, core reactions and emotions. The limbic system controls basic emotions such as fear, anger, and pleasure, and drives hunger, sex, dominance, and care of offspring. These deep, instinctual emotions and drives are part of body consciousness and can operate completely separate from, and in opposition to, higher emotions and thought processes; they are what is called in yoga, "animal consciousness."

As aspiring yogis, we often come up against the operation of these lower parts of the brain and it drives us to action that runs contrary to our goals as yogis. We must become masters over these lower impulses. If we are driven by these basic impulses, we will be ignorant of higher brain reasoning and the intuition of Divine Consciousness.

There are two basic ways for attaining mastery over these lower forces. These may be used in tandem. The first is through a strong mental will keeping the mind on God, and the second is through dispassionate observation. James said, "Submit yourself, and then to God, and resist the devil and he shall flee from you, come near to God and he will come near you" (James 4:7). Then Jesus said, "But I tell you, resist not an evil person" (Matthew 5:39). One may interpret these two sayings to say: Firmly turn your mind away from evil, putting your full attention on God (and the contrary impulses will leave you), and the second is to be the dispassionate observer, giving no power to evil.

There are two instances that have recently come to me. One happened earlier this week and the other occurred a week and a half after I had the operation. After I had the tumors removed and was in recovery, I experienced three days of a deep grief welling up inside of me. It was the body grieving for what it had recently undergone. I observed the grief flowing through me—moving through until it finally expended itself. My mind was clear as the emotions came up. I felt myself watching the grief, like a river flowing through me.

The second occurrence happened this past week. I had traveled back to the Northwest and received the vaccination that had been prepared for me. The vaccination had nothing but my own cells: tumor cells that had been sterilized and my own white blood cells. But body consciousness was triggered by the vaccination that included tumor cells (even though they were sterilized); a strong feeling of not wanting tumors to grow again came bubbling up from someplace deep inside of me.

When I told Carla of this reaction, she said the vaccination had not only tumor cells, but also the white blood cells, the good guys. She thought of the white blood cells as Hanuman and the millions of monkeys and bears that fought for Rama! This thought made me smile, and a good feeling spread over me; however, this good feeling coexisted with the feeling of dread in the body for the next day and a half. Eventually, the dread left and only the feeling of Hanuman and the millions of monkey-white-blood-cell-warriors continued afterward.

Jesus faced a great trial on the eve of his crucifixion. He knew what was to come, and everything inside of him was demanding, "Oh my Father, if it be possible, let this cup pass from me." Then turning his mind to God in complete surrender, he said, "Nevertheless, not as I will but as Thou wilt" (Matthew 26:39). It is at this point of total surrender that the story comes full circle. It all began when Adam and Eve went against Divine Will, giving into the serpent force for their own pleasure and the promise that they should not die (Genesis 3:4). This error by Adam and Eve (reason and feeling) is rectified when the son of man totally gives himself to Divine Will for certain suffering and death, as well as for eventual resurrection and glory.

We can trace our own journey of going out from God, when we too choose to go against God's inner direction and become subject to the primitive components of the brain—no longer living by Higher Consciousness alone. Once those lower impulses come alive, they dominate our thinking, and we enter into the great ignorance: maya and avidya.

Our way back is through dispassion toward the lower impulses, keeping our full attention upon God, and being in complete surrender to His will. Jesus demonstrated this in his own life, as do all the fully realized spiritual masters. We follow in the great one's footsteps and are flawlessly led to our eternal oneness with our Divine Mother and Heavenly Father.

March 25

UNBOUNDED FREEDOM

Full Moon.**

For those with eagle-hearts, confinement to a limited body consciousness is too imprisoning, too suffocating to endure. Fortunately, we may learn to soar in spiritual skies and experience unbounded freedom, even as we yet remain living in the body.

Last night in our Kriya class, we explored that endless freedom. It starts with the mind's power to create images, or imagination. Imagination is often derided as a false reality. And, it is a fact that some can imagine many things, both true and false, and call them all true. But that should not take away from the reality that imagination can create a doorway to higher Reality; imagination is not that higher Reality, but it can trigger a true experience.

We started with what we were aware of in our normal conscious experience, ourselves in our bodies. Then closing our eyes, we were aware of our breathing, for breathing is a vital part of our body-mind-spirit connection. As we breathed, we inwardly saw our spirits expand beyond just the body and felt ourselves grow out to the auric field, about arm's length out, all around the body (imagine this for yourself even as you read this). We felt that we were expanded to that degree and we experienced that vitality, the peace, and the Light of our Being was now larger.

Then we expanded out to the size of the room we were in, and all the people in that room. Gradually we continued to grow, and identified with the community we were in, and saw that the spirit of light, love, peace, and bliss were permeating all that we encompassed. Then we saw ourselves beholding this world as if looking at it from a distance, and that Satchidananda (pure being, conscious-awareness, and bliss) was saturating the earth and all its beings.

We continued further to expand out to encompass the solar system, then the galaxy, and island galaxies, even out to this entire universe, and island universes, and the vast Astral Realm beyond material creation; then (if we dared!), we could encompass the much more expanded field of the Causal Realm, and finally into the unlimited Spirit of God. And from there, to remember what it was like to be limited to the little body, how tiny and cramped this was in comparison to the vast expansion of Spirit.

No wonder we balk at the notion that the body and the material world are all that we are. And it also makes it understandable why souls get lost along the way and use drugs and alcohol in a vain attempt to experience that great freedom (and what a poor and dangerous imitation that attempt is!).

Afterward, even while driving the car home, I continued in that expanded state of mind, and I told those in the car, "Not bad driving for one who is still out amongst the stars!" I had only a toehold on the body, enough to operate safely here on earth. And now, in the early morning hours, my spirit continues to soar in the freedom of endless expansion and bliss.

We all can merge thinking into Being with practice and purification, and oh, what we may become as we explore our true Being! Can you not sense the call of freedom tugging at you—an open breeze that seeks to fill the sails of your spirit and take you into unending Bliss? It can start with your imagining this reality unfurling those closed tight sails, then entering the doorway and finding yourself moving into the Reality of the freedom-loving Divinity within you, and all about you. Even now, do you not hear the call?

Health Update: With practice, one can move from oceanic consciousness to the little pond of body consciousness, without losing the freedom of the eternal Self. So, to shift subjects, this body continues to feel perfect recovery. Blood tests show that I am on the cusp of no longer being anemic; I do not notice any current signs of fatigue from the previous very low blood numbers.

I received my first vaccine injection that only contains my own cells, a combination of sterile tumor cells along with concentrated white blood cells. Other than some tiredness in the afternoon since the injection was received, I have had no other reaction. The idea is to target the immune system onto those cancerous cells in the early stages of formation. This is the second phase of the study for this vaccination. In the first phase (a test of a fewer number of participants), the three or four participants who had stage four cancer and had these injections have not had a recurrence of tumors. The few numbers of people in this category are not conclusive, but encouraging.

I have consulted one of the nation's best oncological naturopaths and he said that melanoma is the top cancer for being responsive to naturopathic treatment. He took blood samples and I will meet with him again in a couple of weeks. In the meantime, he recommends eating large servings of vegetables, half of a plate of food are vegetables, a palm size amount of protein, and a half to a cup of complex carbohydrates (such as quinoa). Use the Vitamix daily to liquefy an apple, a carrot, and a mixture of green vegetables, whatever is in the fridge, such as kale. Also, he has prescribed large doses of curcumin in capsule form, some other supplements, and suggested I drink Sei Mee green tea, whose ground leaves are equal to 20 cups of ordinary green tea in antioxidant power. He will have other recommendations after he gets the results from the blood tests.

In the meantime, I feel the vitality of perfect health, and most of all, of course, God and Guru's grace continues to fill me with the unbounded freedom of the Divine Presence.

March 27

RESURRECTION

Empty Tomb in Nazareth.**

On this Easter morning, we mark the resurrection of Jesus of Nazareth. In the dictionary, we read the definition of resurrection: the act of causing something that had ended or been forgotten or lost to exist again, to be used again. In the telling of the life of Jesus, it is the physical ending of his life when crucified upon a wooden cross and then his miraculous rising back to life.

Resurrection from death is an event that occurs in the vast majority of the world's religions, and it has deep significance for all of us. In a worldly sense, someone may have his career, marriage, or a friendship resurrected after, to all appearances, it had ended or died. Emotionally and psychologically, we may have resurrection when we recover from a trauma and had subsequently died to a meaningful part of ourselves, only to have that part come alive once again.

Spiritually speaking, which is the primary purpose of Easter and the story of Jesus, resurrection takes on an even greater meaning. While the above-mentioned resurrections are deeply significant to a person's life, they pale in comparison to the spiritual dimension for you and for me.

We know from the scriptures that Jesus went through many profound experiences before he came to the crucifixion. He was baptized by John the Baptist, and God's voice proclaimed him His son, and as a Light broke over him, he was tempted in the desert and overcame all obstacles; he selflessly served humanity through healings, teachings, and on many occasions working to the point of exhaustion, then finding renewal in isolation on a mountain top. These are just a few of the glimpses we have of the master from the writings that have been preserved.

All of these experiences are leading to a kind of grand finale, a moment of great transformation. From the time Jesus consciously and voluntarily puts himself into harm's way by returning to Jerusalem, through the moving events of the last supper and his total surrender to God in the Garden of Gethsemane, we follow the master step by step, finally leading to his crucifixion. Through Mother and Master, we know that this description is the symbolic story of every aspirant as he or she seeks transformation from the human to the Divine.

Thus, the inner or Mystical Crucifixion is a specific set of experiences everyone can expect to go through in their own spiritual ascent when the time is right. Resurrection occurs after the soul has gone through the crucifixion experiences necessary to purify body, mind, and soul.

From death in the heart center, a blocking stone is rolled away, leading to a resurrection in which Divine Love now flows through the heart from an unending Source. Death in the fifth chakra, the throat center, purifies the Astral/electrical body of all impurities, and now truth and radiance shine from the inner soul.

Ascending to the Causal sixth center, the Christ Center, a resurrection of the pure intelligence of God now flows through the brain, bringing Light, Truth, and Love from sacred Omniscience—God the Father. And finally, complete death, not just of the body, but of the all-human sense of a separate self, leads to the ascendancy of a son of man to becoming a Son of God; nay, more than that, the resurrection of God-hood.

This resurrection, as you will surmise, is not just for one man who lived two thousand years ago but is the story of every individual making this ascendancy. Jesus **is** the way, the truth, and the life; he leads you in the Way that completely transforms your life. It may come as a comfort for some to think that Jesus did all the heavy lifting and they can just ride along on his coattails. However, for the intrepid soul who recognizes the truth, resurrection **must** be a deeply meaningful transformation in his or her own life. The life of Jesus is a road map for the resurrection of Divine Consciousness in the sincere aspirant.

There **has** been something that has been forgotten—it is God-experience. There **is** something that has been lost—it is the realization of your eternal Self that is ever-conscious and is bliss itself. The resurrection of this state-of-Being means that it once again exists in your life in all of its fullness and glory. It is now for you to use it to help others achieve that same risen state. Easter is here to remind each one of us of this great and central Truth.

April 2

KRIYA INITIATION

Mother Hamilton, 1974 Kriya Initiation.

Kriya Yoga Initiation is a blessed and remarkable occurrence. Every religion across the globe has initiation rites, each one designed to impart spiritual power and transformation. In the yoga tradition, the teacher, or guru, is held in high esteem and unlike some religious movements, you are not simply joining an organization or movement but forming a sacred bond with a living master.

This past week's Kriya Initiation brought to mind my Initiation from Mother Hamilton. I met Mother in March of 1974, soon after my twentieth birthday. After an intense search for a living teacher, I found Mother in ways that on the outside could seem accidental, through a friend of a friend, but now I understand the pull of the guru differently. Mother was not what I was expecting; I was thinking more along the lines of a wizened Indian man with a grey beard and long hair if I had to put an image to it. In fact, I had met such venerable-looking gurus, but I did not feel the connection I was looking for. Although Mother was not the image I had in mind, she was more of a towering spiritual figure than I ever thought possible.

Mother gave Kriya Initiation that following June and I felt privileged and honored to be among the new initiates. Unknown to me at the time, Mother had not given Kriya Initiation for the previous seven years. What eager anticipation I had as I arrived early. I had planned to meditate across the street from the chapel where we were to meet on the beautiful University of Washington campus. It was a very warm and perfect June day.

As I pulled up to the Chapel, another car pulled in behind mine. It was none other than Mother and a devotee, much to my surprise. I offered to help; I brought items into the Chapel and helped set things up. I was allowed to help to a certain point, and then Mother asked me to leave. Afterward, I sat under the blooming trees on the campus and I felt the beauty of the day.

I joined some devotees sitting in the waiting room meditating, and then the number of devotee-bees quickly grew. I wondered what was going to happen during initiation. I knew nothing about initiations, other than I very much wanted to be there. Toward the end of this most amazing ceremony, Mother blessed me with a powerful touch at the ajna, the point between the eyebrows. Later she asked me what I thought about Kriya, and since all the instructions were oral only and I had been anxious that I would be able to remember them all, I said in relief that it was simpler than I had feared.

She instantly rejoined, "Just wait." Of course, she was perfectly right!

The next morning, I vividly remember spreading my woolen blanket on the ground, facing east as the sun slowly revealed itself over the horizon announcing a new day. Indeed, it was a new day! I felt such peace and contentment in practicing this remarkable method for Self-realization, that came from such an ancient tradition, handed down to us through this most amazing guru-lineage. The breath flowed along with the life-current; I was so happy at last to be absorbed in this sacred technique.

It is a mystery how Mother called me to her. It is a mystery how someone such as myself with an ordinary Western background should respond to Eastern teachings that also embody Christianity and the essence of all religious practice. All of it is a great and wonderful mystery. I look back on that moment of Kriya Initiation over forty years ago with incredible gratitude for the gift Mother gave to me. I more fully realize now that my Initiation came at a great price to Mother, in a way that I did not know at the time. My gratitude, my understanding, and my love have only grown with time; forever they shine brightly like the sun, growing and growing in the new morning's light.

April 3

ALL IS HE

Surrounded by Saints: Swami Satchidananda and Swami
Chidananda of Divine Life Society, Anandashram, 1999.

Papa says chanting Ram Nam is sweet, like candy in the mouth. In fact, no words can describe the Bliss felt when chanting God's holy Name. You may say that God has no name that can be spoken with the human tongue, and it is also true that every name is His name. However, there are certain names of God—in all languages—that have been surcharged through sacred repetition that has lifted up saints into the highest Consciousness, like a trail that has been blazed through the wilderness by thousands of years and thousands of feet that wear even sharp stones to smoothness. Ram Nam auspiciously qualifies as one of the most ancient and well used of such incantations.

It is God-experience alone that is the true Name of God: seeing the sacred Light, hearing the soaring AUM or AMEN, feeling the uplifting currents in the spine and brain, and expanding into infinite Spirit. Like a symphony orchestra, God can be the power of a violent storm or the sweetest touch of a spring breeze upon soft petals; God-experience encompasses all experience and is far beyond ordinary perception.

When I was a truck driver, I drove mile after mile chanting the holy Name of Ram Nam. God lifted me up; my eyes partially closed, leaving only enough consciousness in the world to operate the truck. Sometimes, He completely closed my eyes and took me up into pure Spirit with a rush of Bliss and Power in the spine; then, of course, I had to pull over and park on the side of the road!

It took time and many experiences, but gradually the blockages were removed, so that now there is only the pure flow up the spine, the Name of God as AUM resounds all around, God's thoughts flow through my own, His Love animates my heart, and His life-force walks and talks through this form. Far from creating ego, this experience makes me absolutely know that of myself I am nothing, truly nothing. It is He, it is He, it is all He! Where is there room for ego when that is the case?

Oh, what a love-affair God has created. He makes us journey far away from Him in consciousness. Then, He draws us back to Himself, creating magnetism when the time is right that we cannot, and do not want to, resist. In this moment, it is He who writes these words, and it is He who reads them, and it is He who charges them with His uplifting power to draw those He has chosen to Himself. What a wonderful play He has enacted!

When there is nothing but He, what is there to fear? If He wants a certain thing to happen, nothing can stop it. If He wants something not to happen, nothing can make it so. Our trying to go it alone is His trial in ignorance; our surrender to Him is His movement in time and space that purifies creation. Our part is to witness what He does within and all about us.

It may be that these words make no sense to you, and that is His will. It may be that you feel He is speaking these very words directly to, and through you, and that is His will as well. Many times, I hear or see the words of a great master, such as Mother, Master Yogananda, or Papa, and I feel that the words spoken are my very own, for He makes me feel that kind of intimacy with these wonderful human expressions of Himself.

Now, He tells me, it is time to wake up; **it is time for you to wake up!** To feel God weaving Himself through every experience you have in life and to know that it is He alone who exists; One without a second. Why should you suffer separation for one moment longer? There is no reason. He is calling you with His divine magnetism, for it is He, it is He, it is all He; there is nothing else. So, be that! It can all start with chanting His holy Name: Om Sri Ram Jai Ram Jai Jai Ram; Victory to God—Victory to the Light.

April 7

BUILDING A PERFECT HOUSE IN GOD

Yogacharya David and Carla in front of the Taj Mahal, 2013.

t is springtime and there is a building boom going on in our neighborhood. Not only is Jerry and Lois' house coming to completion, but there are four other houses being built nearby. Other than design differences, there are noticeable distinctions in the quality of materials and craftsmanship in each one. Our mail lady is a self-appointed evaluator of such quality, saying Jerry and Lois' home is very high quality, unlike their neighbors! Ram's fun.

Whatever part you play in life, there are principles of high-quality work that will have vastly different results depending on the work ethic you put into it. Whether you are an accountant, a builder of homes, a clerk in a store, a raiser of children, whatever it is, quality definitely counts. And many times, the distinctions are not that noticeable on the outside, but the outcome over time will tell a very different tale.

Oftentimes, one will put effort into one part of life, but ignore the qualities in other parts. This imbalance will show increasing results as time goes on. One may want the latest and greatest television or camera but go into debt to get it, ignore financial health in order to have a passion fulfilled. One may eat only organic natural foods yet smoke cigarettes or marijuana while ignoring the risks and obvious filth that comes with inhaling smoke.

To have a balanced life, we must have high-quality living in all its aspects. We may have a very good professional life but ignore or take for granted home life. We have all had at least some experience with what quality is like. When you handle some fabric that has exquisite craftsmanship, or you closely observe a beautiful flower, or listen to enchanting music, you do not need anyone to explain to you its fineness; you simply know it.

Thinking about applying the principle of quality to all aspects of life, you can immediately identify when it is present and when it is absent. Refining your intuitional sense, the uplifting characteristics are felt deep down. It may be when you meet someone, see a building, or observe a magnificent landscape, this quality resonates in you at your solar plexus: peaceful, uplifting, and expansive.

Your spiritual practice at once stands alone, and it is also connected with every part of living; it is at the center of your life when you put God first. Spending quality time with God (you know when you have, and you know when you have not) emanates out to all other activities. The feelings of upliftment, peace, love, and joy permeate your entire day, changing its quality because of the state of being you are in, attuning you to bring in more of the highest vibrations based on the choices you make.

Look to the highest quality in every part of your life. You are building a perfect house in God every day of your life. The materials you choose and the care with which you build both increase your satisfaction today and will make a vast difference in your life and the lives of all those you touch as time unfolds. Create with the uplifting quality of God in all you do and experience the difference.

April 9

ASPIRATION VS. ATTACHMENT

Sri Yukteswar with Paramhansa
Yogananda, Calcutta, 1935.**

M oods are a bane to your spiritual life. They are caused by attachment—life is not going the way you think it should. This thought authors an emotion, and oftentimes this feeling is a well-worn track, like a rut on the road that draws an unwary traveler into a direction that gets him or her stuck.

Moods can be of two types: a rajasic mood, in which anger comes with cutting thoughts and sharp words and you slash your way through the day. The other type is tamasic, a depressive mood that hangs around you like a dark cloud, allowing no light to penetrate. Either or both of these moods can dominate the mind and bring the sadhaka to a dead end.

While having a reaction to life's events can happen in a blink of an eye, and the body and mind can have momentary shock, there is a time limit when that reaction will simply dissipate. Then there are those times when you nurse a feeling, adding new energy for diverse purposes that will extend those feelings and create a mood.

You may have an expectation that life should be different: easier, more prosperous, smoother relationships, healthier, kinder, etc. It is not that these are not perfectly good aspirations to have in life, but to be attached to these aspirations creates a mood; hanging on to that mood brings you down, undoubtedly bringing others down as well.

Master said that Sri Yukteswar warned him about becoming moody and having an unregulated life. Perhaps these are connected, moods being a result of unregulated thinking. We generally think of moods as being an emotion, yet they originate in the reasoning mind, as we first entertain an idea of how life should be versus how it is.

Using jnana, discrimination, you surgically remove or cancel the expectation that life should be different. This does not mean you do not aspire to something better; however, you cut out the expectation. Do you see the difference? For that difference is crucial. Expectation is attachment. Aspiration ties into creativity. Attachment binds you to this world. Aspiration lifts you up and when done properly, unites you with higher consciousness.

It is compassion that wants a better world. You see the suffering in this world and have aspirations for healing, holiness, happiness, and health for one and for all. A prayerful state of mind makes you look out to the world from the eyes of God; divine energy flows out from your heart as in a compassionate living river. You then feel prompted into action to alleviate the suffering of another. Part and parcel of this attitude is the peaceful joy that flows throughout your being.

In contrast, when you have an attachment to the idea that this world should be better—should just work better, be more equal, just, etc., that attachment will make you feel angry or depressed when you see the poor state this world is in. Anger prompts cutting words left, right, and center for the villains, or you withdraw from this world into a dark mood. Neither of these responses connects you with higher consciousness; rather, they create doubt in there being anything higher than the suffering you see.

In both of these examples, the world is exactly the same; however, aspiration is freeing, attachment binds you. You must be a careful guardian of your thoughts and feelings in order to have true freedom. While a dark thought or feeling can erupt in a micro-second, it is likely that there has been a build-up period coming for a time—a preceding lack of intensity in your sadhana. Constant remembrance of God frees you. Forgetfulness binds you. It is a simple formula, and it determines your taking the higher road to true and lasting happiness.

April 15

ENLIGHTENED SELF-INTEREST

Mother Hamilton with Saint Teresa of Calcutta:
Two great Servants of God, India, 1977.

Normally, our interests lie very close to home; we are mostly interested in what will satisfy our senses and the ego. Through the evolution of consciousness, we grow to want what is best for our family, circle of friends, perhaps our hometown, and even our country. Through this enlarging circle, we can see the gradual expansion of interest, heart, and spirit.

Entering into a spiritual understanding of life makes you know there is no part of life that is not connected to the whole, or to yourself. Compassion arises in the soul when the interest of another becomes important to you. It may be the suffering of a child, an animal, or a group of people that are not normal members of your circle of association. You find yourself sacrificing for others without thought of reward for yourself, just as saints around the world have spent themselves in such service to humanity.

However, one can be of service to others from two vastly different motivations. Initially, service can be for the aggrandizement of the ego, "Look what I have sacrificed for others; no, I mean it—**look** at what I have done for others." Or, sacrifice and service are driven by what is satisfying to God, not motivated by what others think.

We may be misled by the word sacrifice, thinking there is no satisfaction in it and that we must simply suffer. This notion comes from the mental conditioning of the ego. In reality, in harmonizing your life with God there is a transfer from self-interest, which creates suffering, to an enlightened Self-interest, which brings systemic harmony and joy of service.

Ordinary self-interest is driven by the needs of the body and the ego-mind. It can be the narrow self-interest of a child in order to satisfy his or her needs for food, warmth, comfort, and the developing needs of an ego. Ordinary self-interest can also be the more intricate calculations for gaining wealth, power, and prestige in the world: always the needs are driven by the body and the ego-mind.

Enlightened Self-interest comes from a wider identification with creation—seeing the world through the mind of the Creator. Looking out upon the world, there is no perceived difference between the happiness of others and yourself. True Self-interest is not calculated for doing some good, rather it is a spontaneous response to the collective needs of creation that spring from an intuitive understanding of the Creator's will.

Real Self-interest is not attached to outcomes; it does not care who sees or does not see and it feels spontaneous joy in performing the activity itself. True Self-interest gives joy to the giver as well as the receiver. There is no "martyrdom complex" in which the giver must suffer alone; rather, giving is an expression of Divine Will and therefore brings total freedom to the servant of God.

In God-consciousness, all humankind and all creation are part of you, and you feel joy at the physical, mental, and spiritual progress of creation. You also feel pain at the suffering and mistakes of those who are none other than your Self. God's compassion flows through you and you feel the all-encompassing Divine Comforter inter-mixed with tender, even painful, compassion for others.

The Divine Presence in you now naturally radiates out of you to uplift and heal creation of its suffering. We all broadcast what we experience in life to those whom our lives touch. Being in tune with the Divine Presence increases the power of what you transmit, bringing solace, beauty, and purity to this world. God uses you to broadcast His love and compassion to all creation! There is truly nothing more useful or deeply meaningful for you than to lead a life of true Self-interest.

April 21

A BRIDGE TO THE INFINITE

Bridge to the Light.**

L ife throws so many experiences at us from unexpected directions. From the time we are little children and our world is
full of adult knees to the time when we look in the mirror
and wonder who that old person is staring back at us—life is a
roller coaster ride of experiences!

What is this life all about? It is a question that makes us go
deeper than just living on the surface. The quest for meaning can
be the beginning of the greatest adventure in life—the search for
God-realization.

In this venture into higher consciousness, we are told to keep
our minds on God as a means of purifying the mind and gaining a

direct perception of the Truth. What we find in doing so is that life rudely interrupts our best intentions for this practice. Earning a living, our social relationships, the desires of the body, and distractions of the world, those thousands and thousands of big and little situations that draw the mind everywhere except to God. It seems that life itself conspires to stop our making real spiritual progress.

In part, the problem is that we imagine these distractions are not part of our practice; we would be so much better off if we could somehow just get rid of them. However, a little analysis reveals that these are not things that keep us from our path; they are the path itself. We have been conditioned to think of all these distractions as something different from God. They are not. In truth, they are God come to us in these various forms.

At last, you come to terms with the fact that when it comes to daily life, its distractions and its desires are really dynamic expressions of Divine Consciousness. When you have understood this, you have found a key to understanding life in a new and transformative way. The life-energy and intelligence found in all life, even life that apparently runs contrary to elevated consciousness, all come from one original Source.

A way to reconnect to this universal vision in which *all is God* is to allow all input into your brain, let all thoughts and all feelings remind you of God. In your mind, you create a bridge to God with each and every experience. For instance, a beautiful sunset reminds you of God; that is an easy one. Then you think of the food you eat as ingesting God; this is more unusual, but you can work with it. Tougher categories come as sexual drives, an impulse to lie, fear creeping into your awareness, and anger erupting; looked at properly, all of these lower impulses can become bridges back to God. However, since these thoughts have taken you in the opposite direction from God in the past, they represent an even bigger stretch for you in your practice.

By connecting a thought or feeling to God, you break the spell of separation. For example, take the sensation of pain. It can definitely be a distraction; even the thought of having pain in the future can take the mind far from God-consciousness. You build a bridge to God by thinking of the life-energy that is in the pain impulse itself; that life-energy gives the electrical impulse its power to travel to your brain via nerve pathways. By connecting to the life-energy that is behind the pain impulse and affirming that the life-energy comes from God—you are directing your mind directly back to its ultimate Source, and, as a result, you feel greater strength, peace, and an ability to weather any storm coming your way.

Another example: you are feeling a sexual drive that is drawing you away from God. You then sense the power of God as the energy behind the drive. This bridge to God you are making releases the purity of God, you realize how limiting the sex impulse is, how narrowly it focuses your mind and you suddenly feel a release from it and an expansive freedom. You can do the same with fear, anger, depression, and the feeling of being overwhelmed; all situations can be bridged back to the Infinite, thus connecting you to all the attributes of Spirit and freeing you from the limitations imposed by the separation from your higher Self.

Keeping your mind on God then becomes practical and is rooted in your day-to-day experience. It creates a magic touch when your lower impulses receive Grace and are transformed into something higher, better. This "Midas touch" does not make ordinary objects turn into metallic gold; rather, ordinary experience is touched by transformative Spirit and becomes the gold of God-consciousness. Take heart, you are not left helpless against an onslaught of materialism; rather, you have the means to connect with God in all circumstances and thus build a bridge to the Infinite.

Health Note: The result of my last CAT and PET scans found that there is a mass on my liver that is 2 cm by 2 cm. A biopsy will be performed on Thursday at 4 p.m. to determine the nature of the mass. The time required for the procedure will be one hour, and I will be in the hospital for a total of five hours, including prep time beforehand and observation afterward.

I deeply appreciate all the prayers, long-distance Reiki, and suggestions for optimizing health you have so lovingly given me. I continue with the program the oncological Naturopath has pre-scribed, both for food and supplements. I have also received two of the six injections for the vaccine that has been made with my own body cells. I will continue to give you updates as I know more. It is likely, based on past experience, that the biopsy results will be known sometime next week.

April 24

Will and Surrender

Mother Hamilton: A perfect blend
of will and surrender, c. 1967.

Mother spoke powerfully about two seemingly opposite means of dealing with life's problems. One is to use your God-tuned will, as she effectively did, in order to overcome tremendous obstacles, and the second is to surrender to God's will at all times. So, which do you do, fight or surrender?

Confusion comes from the word surrender. Many associate surrender with defeat; this is **not** what is intended when it comes to your sadhana, your spiritual practice. Surrender to God means you are first attuning your mind to God's Mind; if there is a difference between your will and God's, then you go with what God is directing you to do rather than your own inclination.

For instance, lower impulses make you feel that your mind is being drawn away from God. You know the limiting, tortured feelings that come from following these desires. Like a honey trap, you are drawn by the cloying sweet sensations inside the trap, but once you enter in, you are encaged. God-experience frees you from the trap, but you must clearly choose God over sweet, deadly promises.

You may have fear concerning some experience coming your way. Fear disconnects you from God; it builds fear upon fear and will dominate your life; it makes you think of the worst scenarios, and you feel helplessly caught. The fact that you are made in the likeness and image of pure transcendent God-consciousness is completely obliterated by the fog of fear.

Surrender to God means you use your powerful will to focus your mind upon God, not the images of fear. You affirm that God is at the core of your being; it is His Light, courage, strength, mirthful-joy, and love that act as angel wings to lift you above the clouds of doubt and enclosing fear. You concentrate on the truth that God knows whether a sparrow falls, and He has counted the hairs on your head (Matthew 10:29–30); in other words, there is not a single thing that occurs in this wide world that is beyond the knowledge and care of its Creator.

Currently, I am waiting to hear back on the results of the biopsy taken on Thursday. In the waiting, I have a choice of what to focus my mind on: the possibility of tumor growth, or upon God. I know that God is aware of my preference for the test results. I affirm and I think only of having perfect health. I also am surrendered to His will, asking that all be accomplished for the higher Good of all. For me, this is the larger purpose in life; the higher Good is more important than my own preference. Many times, there is no difference between my preference and what is for the higher Good, but then sometimes there is. When there is a difference, I surrender to God's wisdom.

So, in the waiting, I feel I am God's child, totally surrendered to His will. I also think only of perfect health; my body is filled through and through with His Light, all the cells shining in His perfection. No matter the results of this biopsy I will continue this thought of perfection, for it brings me into His Holy Presence in body, mind, and spirit.

I also behold that same Light in you, for it adds prayerful thought-energy to your perfection in Him. Not only is this thought of perfection best for your spiritual health, but it also enacts the highest principle for superior physical health as well. In this way, you use both surrender to God and your powerful will to lift you closer to God, enabling perfect health and giving you peaceful joy!

May 4

Micro-Moments of Joy

Lake Mead bike ride: A micro-moment of joy!

As we make our way back to the Northwest, we have found the journey to be smooth and delightful. After some busy days before leaving, then flying down here and preparing the motorhome for travel—retrieving it from its dusty storage—we made our way back to a place we enjoyed before near Wickenburg Arizona. The quiet of the desert is much preferred to staying at an RV park where units are stacked like cordwood.

The next day, we motored north to another familiar campground on the shores of Lake Mead, near Hoover Dam in Nevada. We have taken a day from travel to take a bike ride along a railroad line that has been converted into a trail, complete with tunnels under mountains and vistas of Lake Mead. We do have a schedule to keep in order to make it back in time for more doctor appointments. These appointments will point the way to another surgery and a probable course of treatment for the new tumor that was found on the liver.

In spite of a looming future and a schedule of travel to be mindful of, we have found joy in the journey. I have no real thoughts for these future events other than making calls and texting doctors and caregivers that need occasional promptings. Although I have been impressed with the speed and care of treatment, still it has required a sometimes steady stream of promptings to busy providers to keep things moving along properly.

So, while future events may provide plenty of reasons to be distracted, be in a mood, or spend time worried, I have found none of this to be my experience. Rather, there are innumerable sparks of joy—too many to count. Packed within each day, discreet situations bring fulfillment, happiness, and connection with God. I have thought of these as micro-moments of joy.

These micro-moments of joy do not need to be extraordinary in any way. They can be simply driving down the road, feeling the warmth in the air, seeing a hummingbird tasting the nectar of a flower, or a vista of lovely desert mountains. If I were obsessed with the future or stressed by a schedule to keep, or any number of reasons to be distracted from the here and now, I would surely miss these micro-moments of joy.

These micro-moments are available to all, but all too often our eyes do not see and our ears do not hear. Life is full of joyful moments, but how impoverished is the person who cannot enjoy them. It makes life dull and meaningless when there is no joy, or when that joy is always deferred to a hoped-for, better future. God **is** joy, and unless we are actively participating in joy, then we are starving our soul of the very nourishment it absolutely needs.

No matter your situation, you have available to you these micro-moments of joy. Do not let moods, concerns, fears, or unbridled desires make you deaf and blind to everyday joy. Your meditation is designed to bring out that joy. God remembrance is joy itself, and such joy is not dependent upon wealth, health, or situation—for God is transcendent to all such considerations. Jesus even proclaimed, blessed is he who mourns, for he shall be comforted. Comforted by whom? Comforted by God who is to be found in the hearts of all, and God who comes to you in all the various forms He may choose to send.

Do not rob yourself of the present by banking all of your hopes upon an uncertain future or holding today under a microscope of what you think it should look like. You are a creature of joy, designed to live in bliss. Look for those moments today, now. Find micro-moments of joy all through the day, string these moments together and make a beautiful pearl necklace of God-joy. As the great Meher Baba exhorted us to do, "Don't worry, be happy!"

May 8

MOTHER'S DAY

Hindu Goddess Durga Ma riding tiger.**

W e honor mothers everywhere for all that they do to make life itself possible, for their special brand of love that acts as a balm for the hurts and disappointments of life, and for all that they give in selfless service so that all may have happiness.

Our mothers are expressions of the Divine Mother. Here in the West, we are not so prone to think of God as Divine Mother due to Jesus' special emphasis on his Abba, his heavenly Father. But Jesus also spoke of the Holy Ghost, and in Aramaic (the language of Jesus), She is feminine. Jesus spoke of the Comforter, of the Holy Ghost bringing truth, but also as the name implies, She also comforts the soul. Even though the emphasis down through time has not been on the Divine Mother, still the basis is there in the original teachings of Jesus.

In the East, the Divine Mother plays a much more prominent role. Many of the images in India of the Divine Mother are fierce, such as Durga riding upon a tiger and holding a sword, and Kali is forbidding with skulls and a bloody tongue. Symbology is rich here, but in the end, devotees such as Ramakrishna testify that when you bravely enter into the mystery of the Divine Mother, behind the fierceness, the Mother is beautiful beyond compare—and so loving.

We can draw a lesson from this transformation from the fierce to a loving expression of the Divine Mother. This world is an expression of Divine Mother (Mother Nature). Oftentimes, this world is a fierce place to live; there are hardships and pain, challenges, and a lack of harmony. When the nature of this world is bravely faced, we see behind the mask of duality the loving expression of the Divine Mother who ever seeks to comfort us and who assures us of Her love.

Master wrote of the extreme pain he felt at the passing of his mother when he was yet just a boy. Through the power of his devotion and the grace of Master Mahasaya, Divine Mother appeared to him, and in Her eyes, he saw his own mother's eyes of love and compassion. Divine Mother told young Mukunda that it was She who loved him through his earthly mother, and She would love him always.

Papa Ramdas also had a powerful relationship with Divine Mother. As he wandered across India penniless and exposed to the elements, he thought of his Ram as Divine Mother who would look to his every need and be a comfort to him on his bold travels. He drew strength from thinking of God as Mother, and She was a solace to him in every need.

So, today I honor my own mother for the steadfast loving care she demonstrated in life. My heart melts when I think of so many expressions of Divine Mother—I see loving and caring for the children of new generations, and for those ladies who have not had children, yet are great expressions of Divine Mother in love and compassion for so many. I bow at the feet of my own Gurudev, who is the true embodiment of Divine Mother. And, thinking on the Divine Mother, I am instantly filled with Her loving, blissful nature. In truth, there is no difference between Divine Mother in her universal form and her expressions through Her human forms—for through Her touch all transform into Her very Self.

These are my early morning thoughts as I contemplate in love and gratitude the Divine Mother in Her universal expression, and in Her human loving kindness. Infinite blessings to all Mothers.

Roses for the Divine Mother in You.

May 15

PRAYAG

The Snake and Columbia Rivers Prayag.

Prayag is a term from India that means "place of offerings." It most often denotes the confluence of rivers (a Sangam), such as Allahabad, where the Ganga, Yamuna, and the invisible Saraswati rivers come together.

On our Pilgrimage trip back to the Northwest, we stopped at a North American prayag, where the Snake River meets the Columbia River. So many times, we ascribe great meaning to sacred places that are in distant locations. It is not that such places do not deserve our reverence, but we can overlook those sacred spots that are close by.

A favorite pilgrimage spot for me in India is Rudra Prayag, as the Ganga makes its way down from the Himalayas. There is a sweet temple at the point of confluence at Rudra Prayag, and we had a powerful spiritual feeling on its banks. We had a similarly powerful experience at the confluence of the Snake and Columbia rivers.

A wonderful peace and powerful spiritual vibrancy filled the air. A beautiful park by the name of Sacajawea had the shade of trees, cool green grass, and a small but wonderful museum that exalted the superior character of Sacajawea who acted as guide for the Lewis and Clark expedition. Truly, she had exceptional traits and was a harbinger of peace as the explorers made their way across the continent.

The park was quiet when we were there, and we felt refreshed after some long hours/days of travel just by spending some time there. Part of the purpose of embarking on this North American Pilgrimage is to discover sacred places, both of Nature and human-made.

You may have places close by that are healing, regenerating, and very uplifting that you may or may not have recognized or to which you may not have paid recent homage. Do yourself a favor and seek out those sacred places and receive their blessings, as well add your blessings to them from your uplifted state of mind. Some places in Nature are simply spiritually charged; there may be spots where saints and those of high consciousness imbued them with vibrational power, and then there are those spots that have become pilgrimage spots where, over many years, pilgrims have added their consciousness to an already powerful place.

May you be blessed in seeking out those places where you are spiritually quickened and find peace and healing simply by being open to their beneficent and harmonious vibrations.

Aum, Peace, Bliss, Amen.

May 18

INNER PRAYAG

Prayer offering at the River
Ganges, Varanasi, India.**

Pilgrimage spots are wonderful for traveling to, and becoming immersed in, the uplifting vibrations to be found there: such as where sacred rivers join together. However, in truth, everything we need to have the highest God-experience is to be found within.

The mountain of uplifted consciousness can be known through mystical experience; the ocean of expansive, unending Spirit you may have in deepened meditation; the purity of the clean desert vibration already exists for those who have eyes to see and ears to hear, and the prayag of two rivers becoming one happens right within you.

Allahabad India is where there is a confluence of two rivers, the Ganga and the Yamuna, along with the mythical river Saraswati. This confluence (Sangam), since ancient times, has been called Prayag (a place of offerings). There is an exact correspondence of these physical features found right within your subtle body which reveals the inner kingdom of heaven.

Yoga tradition posits that on either side of the spinal column there are two intertwining currents of life-energy. These currents start at the base of the spinal column, the tailbone area, and travel up to the base of the skull; from there, they run through the brain and end at the point between your eyebrows, the ajna or third eye point.

The two channels of energy represent the pairs of opposites, heat and cool, positive and negative, etc. A third current is singular and runs up the middle of the spinal column and is called the sushumna. In Kriya Yoga, we work with these two energies to bring them into total balance and raise the kundalini or vital spiritual power through the central channel from the base of the spine to the third eye point.

These three currents, the ida, the pingala, and the sushumna correspond to their physical counterparts as the Ganga, Yamuna, and Saraswati rivers. When these three currents merge at the third eye point, your full attention is riveted on the ajna, you see a brilliant shining Light. The power of this confluence makes one sail through the triumvirate colors of the third eye and individual consciousness merges with the Infinite.

Prayag means place of offering; it is the place at the ajna where you offer yourself and all that you call your own at the feet of God. In this complete surrender, you qualify to become one with pure Divinity. It is here that your entire spiritual practice and pilgrimage in life find fulfillment. By repeatedly subsuming all that you are into the oceanic bliss of God, you are purified of every limitation. It is God Himself who takes you by the hand and makes you a fit offering for this rite of total transformation.

Your life is no longer your own as God expresses Himself through you. For the true devotee, there is nothing else he or she wants in life but to be God's, and God's alone. Every moment of your life, you feel His power, bliss, and intelligence flowing through every part of your Being. The river of individual consciousness originates from the Source of everything that is and is ever running to the sea of All-consciousness! Such is the mystery when man is in God, and God is in man. Achieving this Goal of goals is the result of the confluence and the merging prayag within you.

May 22

The Inner Sound

River flowing.**

I sit next to a rushing river, freshly melted snows feeding the frenzy of snow-white rapids as the water rolls and thunders to an unseen end. As I take in this scene of nature that repeats itself yearly, I also listen to the inner sound of Aum/Amen. There are some distinct parallels between the two sounds, one I hear auricularly with the physical ears, and the second comes from a hidden source and is heard with a more subtle receptor.

Both sounds have multiple tones and frequencies. The river initially comes as a roar, then I pick out many high and low tones, like a symphonic orchestra when the sounds of all the instruments play at once, making for a loud crescendo. With practice, one can selectively pick out the sounds of individual instruments, even when all are playing at once. The inner sound comes as a high-pitched sound and has every other sound embedded in it: highs, lows, tiny variations, and wide ranges.

The first sound comes from the river, a physical source. The second sound, the Aum/Amen has quite a different source. The Aum emanates from the creative principle from which all manifestation comes. The Amen originates from the Divine Consciousness, the Source of all that is. Listening to the Aum takes the mind back to its Source when deeply meditated upon. This Aum/Amen is the Word, the Name of God. It is said that the Name of God and God are one. That is, by meditating upon this Name/Word, this inner sound, the mind dissolves and merges into the Divine Consciousness. Thus, it is worthy to meditate upon the Word of Aum/Amen, the Name of God.

Note: When I was physically weakened with anemia, then in recovery from an operation, God continued to flow through this form: however, the overwhelming power of His Word was gracefully reduced during this time. Since my physical recovery, He has poured the Name once again through this form. The way that He works through this form is that He fills me to overflowing and He directs the uplifting power out to all creation, or to certain people or situations; He definitely directs my mind as to what it should be focused on. If I think on something and He is not willing, He makes it impossible to go further with it. He demands complete and total surrender for this Work—the surrender which I gave to Him long ago. In this way, many times I cannot be with you physically in the way I would like to be, for He has me working for Him in this inner fashion. Know always, I am with you in Spirit. Concentrate on the heart center or the ajna center and we may commune in that beatific Spirit.

June 2

COMPENSATION

Ralph Waldo Emerson, 1857.

Mother Hamilton once said that America produced two great God-realized souls: Ralph Waldo Emerson (1803–1882) and Walt Whitman (1819–1892). Emerson wrote a very interesting article entitled "Compensation." Emerson studied the texts of India as well as the Bible and in this article, he makes reference to both as he discusses the law of compensation, which includes the law of karma, that every action has an equal and opposite reaction. Another topic in the writing is that the whole is embedded in every part. If a part does not exhibit the whole, then it is implied and will eventually be manifest.

He writes:

This law writes the laws of cities and nations. It is in vain to build or plot to combine against it. Things refuse to be mismanaged for long . . . Though no checks to a new evil appear, the checks exist, and will appear. If the government is cruel, the governor's life is not safe. If you tax too high, the revenue will yield nothing. If you make the criminal code sanguinary, juries will not convict. If the law is too mild, private vengeance comes in . . . These appearances indicate the fact that the universe is represented in every one of its particles. Everything in nature contains all the powers of nature. Everything is made of hidden stuff . . . The world globes itself in a drop of dew . . . The true doctrine of omnipresence is that God reappears with all his parts in every moss and cobweb. The value of the universe contrives to throw itself into every point. If the good is there, so is the evil; if the affinity, so the repulsion; if the force, so the limitation.

Thus is the universe alive. All things are moral. The soul which within us is a sentiment, outside of us is the law. We feel its inspiration; out there in history, we can see its fatal strength. 'It is in the world, and the world was made by it.' Justice is not postponed. A perfect equity adjusts its balance in all parts of life. The dice of God are always loaded. The world looks like a multiplication table, or a mathematical equation, which, turn it how you will, balances itself. Take what figure you will, its exact value, not more nor less, still returns to you. Every secret is told, every crime punished, every virtue rewarded, every wrong redressed, in silence and certainty. What we call retribution is the universal necessity by which the whole appears wherever a part appears. If you see smoke, there

must be fire. If you see a hand or limb, you know that
the trunk to which it belongs is there behind. Every act
rewards itself, or, in other words integrates itself . . . [5]

Hidden within any part is the whole. No matter the appearance of things, the balance is implied. We look about us at the terrible things that happen in this world, and we can despair. However, the evil that Adolf Hitler perpetrated must be balanced by the same amount of good. The good that St. Francis enacted will have been preceded by some great calamity. Those we know in this world who seem devoid of wisdom or goodness <u>must</u> have that within them, and the time will come when virtue comes forward; it is the law of creation.

However, this world is not just about balance scales. The dark density of matter is but a shadow of the transcendent Light. In creation, light cannot exist without shadow, but the pure Light of God needs no opposite; it is Self-existent. Our eternal, true nature exists outside of dual forces. The dissatisfaction that ignorance creates must then propel us to enlightenment. Papa Ramdas tells us that the worse things look in this world, the greater will be the impetus to return to God.

There is no doubt that it is much better to stand up straight and walk to the door of Divine Consciousness in wisdom rather than get dragged to that same door with bleeding hands and knees. But return to it we will—for the Divine is part and parcel of our nature and it cannot be forever hidden. It is true for ourselves and for all creation. So, take heart for this world; within each part is the whole of creation, and also that which is beyond creation—the supreme and infinite Creator. We may affirm Mother Hamilton's song's lyrics with all of our hearts:

---

5   www.emersoncentral.com

We all come from God, and in Him we all return. Like a drop of rain, returning to the ocean. Like a ray of light, returning to the sun. Yes, we all come from God.

Health Update: Friday I go in for surgery to remove a tumor and part of the liver, as well as the gall bladder. The surgery will be at 7:30 a.m. and will take three to four hours. The surgeon estimates that I will be in the hospital for three to five days and more complete recovery will require five to six weeks. I continue to feel the power of your prayers, and you are in mine as well. God has given us the great privilege to go to Him together. For that unique opportunity, my heart is filled with loving gratitude.

June 9

IN PERFECT SERVICE

Jesus in perfect service. Catholic parish church of St. Matthaus in Alfter.**

B eing a patient in a hospital reminds one of the importance of the ideal of service. There are perhaps few situations in life in which you are least able to do for yourself as post-op. Supine in a bed, hooked up to various IVs and electrodes, reliant upon nurses and other healthcare providers for everything the body needs means that you certainly appreciate the "service" provided.

I have now had four such hospital experiences in the past eight months. It has been interesting to observe the effects of health care staff upon patients, including myself. Overall, it has been impressive to see the care and expertise that has been evident; however, it has not all been equally excellent.

The nursing staff, the primary caregivers in hospitals, who are positive, friendly, caring, and conscientious have, by far, the best effects. Those who carry into their work the toxicity of their own lives, negative and sharp-edged, are a detriment to their patients. Like the famed driving of Mr. Magoo, who drives his car when he is almost blind, causing mayhem wherever he goes and is seemingly oblivious of it—these servants of health also seem to be unaware or uncaring of the health effects they deliver with tainted attitudes. Those in this category are relatively few in number, but they leave an impression that lingers long after their interactions.

It is a brisk reminder of the importance of right service in all stations of life. Wherever God has delivered you, you are in His service. It may be the work that you do, the family you raise, the conversations you have with others, or lending an extra helping hand when needed. We have thousands of opportunities for service all through the day. Even if you do not go out at all, your very thoughts act as prayers and are in service to the Infinite.

When I was in the waiting rooms, when I went into surgery, and in post-op recovery, I prayed for those around me and all through the hospital. It was a service I could do for Him. In conversation with staff and other patients when walking the corridors, I always made it a point to be positive and uplifting, injecting humor when I could to keep things light.

Master said, "Be a smile millionaire," Papa said, "See God in everyone you meet," Mother Hamilton said, "Keep your mind on God," Mother Teresa said, "Do something beautiful for God," Swami Satchidananda said, "Expand your circle of love daily," Jesus said, "What you have done to the least of these, you have done to me." These great ones in God remind us that every day we can directly do something to improve this world.

In life, everyone has cares that can load them down. Living a life of service carries with it built-in Grace; we feel unburdened through our right attitude. Now love and joy glow at the heart of our service and we are sustained by an all-pervading power. In perfect service, we discover one of the great secrets of living a truly successful life.

Health Update: On Friday, I had a successful operation that removed a tumor on my liver and the gall bladder. The tumor was self-contained and so less of the liver was removed than originally planned. The gall bladder had many more gallstones than thought, emphasizing the need to have it removed.

Day zero is operation day. Carla asked if I might be released by day two, Sunday. The head nurse looked at Carla and said skeptically, "We'll see." Sure enough, by Sunday I had met all the criteria the doctor had set out for release and blessedly went home. The discharge nurse said she had never seen anyone released that early after such an operation. A result, I am sure, in response to your continued prayers.

Recovery is continuing on very well. I thank those who have brought meals and sent flowers and sent messages—I receive all the love that is behind them. It is an unusual sensation to have 10 inches of staples charting a course under my right ribcage, but this lends a compliment to the 8-inch vertical line from the previous surgery (that surgeon used super glue, not staples to keep my insides inside!). I am walking daily and doing some exercises so that I will be fit and fine for performing the wedding for Phyllis and John that I am so looking forward to in a week and a half. Pronams, my deepest love, and blessings to you.

June 12

Ridding World-Addiction

Paramhansa Yogananda with
bouquet sent by Rose and Bob.

It has been interesting to observe how God continues to use this form for His purposes, both in the physical body and in the subtle bodies. We sometimes think that we exist only in one form; for instance, this physical body, to the exclusion of any other at any one time. The truth is, we simultaneously have all bodies available to us at all times; it is just that usually we are focused on the physical form and remain oblivious to the more subtle forms.

In the creation story of the Bible, as with many of the myths from around the world, those first expressions of souls in physical forms were warned not to eat of certain fruits in the midst of the garden. Why, we might ask, would God create forbidden fruits in the first place, knowing the dire consequences of its indulgence? We are told in other phases of creation that God looked upon all creation and found it all good, so how could there be evil lurking?

We can look to everyday examples of food reactions to see how this can work. In Genesis, God is quoted as saying, "I have given you every herb bearing seed, which is upon the face of all the earth, and every tree, which is the fruit of a tree yielding seed; to you it shall be for meat" (Genesis 1:29).

But humankind was not satisfied with just gathering seeds and fruits. They chopped, pounded, and ground the seeds and then baked them, making bread and other creations out of the seeds. They concentrated some forms, combined them, and made new creations. So far, we see no great evil. We know some like the taste of sweetness very much. So, concoctions concentrated the taste of sugar, and those who liked this lost their taste for other foods and wanted only that. Now enters in a lack of balance in the diet, which can lead to weight gain and diabetes: health risks. But sugar is found in the cane and the beet; how can it betray the body?

The reason, of course, is that sugar produces such a powerful pleasure impulse that for some people it so dominates desire nature that balance is thrown out the window and it becomes a compulsion or addiction. We can expand our search and find other compulsions and addictions of the human brain that create a blind search for experiences in life that ends up destroying what is good.

Sex impulse must certainly be on that list. The consequences of ungoverned sex impulses are many, from selecting poor partners to social diseases, unwanted pregnancies, rape, jealous murder, addiction to porn or prostitutes. Scantily clad women, sometimes men, are used to sell everything from cars to cigarettes (odd that the form of a woman would have anything to do with the performance of an automobile). These dominant pleasure impulses in the brain are powerful, and for some, they so dominate the brain that all other healthy considerations lose their appeal.

Enter in the addiction of this physical world itself. We are born into this world as a baby. We initially spend perhaps twenty hours a day asleep, reconnecting with the astral world while we gradually adapt to this physical world. As toddlers and small children, we often have an awareness of subtler realms, but little encouragement is given for these experiences. As the massive sensory input of this world rewards and punishes us, we come fully under its grip, forgetting relations, freedom, and awareness of what we were before coming into this world.

There is nothing wrong with this world, per se; rather, it is the powerful and dominant force it becomes attracting our attention that makes us forget the better, purer, and soul awakening forces inside of us; it narrows our attention to such a miniscule aspect of who we really are, and this makes for the mischief.

We meditate, chant, practice the Presence of God, and read uplifting words that remind us of our greater nature. We must do this, again and again, to draw attention away from this world and to give ourselves God-experience. Now we experience the joy, love, and light of God as a continuous enlightenment that makes us know our body is but a very small expression of the vast Being, that, in truth, we really are. Our body and this world are brought into proper perspective and we excrete the toxins of world-addiction from the pores of our being, freeing our soul.

Now we function with full awareness of the various levels of our Being. The world exists for us, but we know it is the result of larger, more perfect forces. The astral/electrical worlds are with us now, operating in our subtle bodies and giving expression to finer feelings and perceptions. The Causal/idea body is also with us, even more powerful, expanded, and vast beyond knowing, with ideas streaming straight from pure Consciousness. And there is Spirit itself that is at the center of all these other expressions, a Light of intense beauty that has no comparison and no opposite, no beginning and no end: the Light of our own Being. We are aware of any or all of these expressions at any time, but even while we operate in the lower worlds, we never forget who we really are in the greater reality. Thus, we once again become our true Self!

Health Update: Recovery continues to proceed very well. On this day eight, I am off all prescribed medications except a daily injection I give myself as a blood thinner, and I am now taking all the supplements from the naturopath that were temporarily suspended before and after surgery. I walk outdoors three times a day and do up to 15 minutes on the rebounder. I have had no difficulty with digesting anything eaten. I rest quite a few hours during the day, but feel stronger day by day. I will see the surgeon again on Tuesday and hopefully have the staples removed at that time.

A hearty thank-you, for your prayers, flowers, cards, and notes. It means so much to me to receive your love in all these ways and I know it adds to the rapidity of my recovery.

June 18

Slipping Through the Bonds

*Sacred Lotus***

am called to meditate; the messenger is a thrill up the spine, a rarified tingling sensation all around the cranium. I sit and joy bubbles up from deep within; a smile creases itself across my face and love pours out through my eyes. The eyes close—life is lifted up the spine to the point between the eyebrows. Then, it slides through the ajna like it's moving through a super soft silken fabric. A tiny fragment of awareness feels Divine Light unfolding in the brain like so many petals of a rounded lotus. That too recedes and awareness is beyond the body, merging into all-space. No thought encroaches into that realm sublime. Pure awareness, slipping through the bonds of heaven and earth where only resplendent Self exists.

Oh Master, Oh Mother, saints of all religions, this is what you have come to awaken in us. All else is simply stuff of the mind. Oh Lord, You are the moving and motionless Spirit, the author of all that is and so much more. I melt in gratitude. Om Gurus, Om Sri Ram.

June 23

SECLUSION AND RECHARGING

North Cascades Pass: North American Alps.

There are times when the body is in need of recharging. Jesus used to go not only into the mountaintop of his own being, but he also retreated into seclusion on mountaintops and into the wilderness. Master, too, retired to the desert and seclusion. In our regulated schedule of work, it is oftentimes difficult to make for times of seclusion, as even holidays tend to be packed with activity.

The additional challenge is that it is not always easy to make the transition to seclusion when we have been active. We tend to take the busyness of the body as a matter of fact, and when we do take time out, the mind continues to wear us out with reviewing the past or rehearsing the future. How difficult, and how valuable to spend time in the here and now, in quiet and seclusion; yet, how rare are the times when we actually do this.

After this past hospitalization and continued recovery, and the many other demands God puts me through, this body is in need of restoration. It is interesting to note that life-energy flows fully through and around this body, but the physical body can feel as a limp rag. It is clear, it needs a rest.

Nature is one of the great restorative agents for the body. Carla too needs a break after her one hundred percent attention to the needs of this body before, during, and after the stay in the hospital and all the other demands on her time and energy. This is not only a long way of saying we have escaped to the wilderness, but it is also a reminder that we all benefit from times of quiet seclusion.

We have set our sights on Glacier National Park, reputed to be one of the scenic wonders of the world. Already, we have camped next to the Skagit River near New Halem and are traveling over the North Cascades Pass, known as the "Alps of North America."

I will keep in touch through these discourses, and you are invited to come along in Spirit as we travel these highways and bi-ways in further pilgrimage to Nature's Cathedrals. As I write these words, my spirit spreads out and floods all-space, and in this spirit, I feel the great Spirit in me in touch with you. Love is the hallmark of this Spirit, the love that is God, a love that knows no bounds.

June 26

SUPERIOR CHARACTER

Sacagawea's Birthplace in Salmon, Idaho.**

I have been reading a historical novel about the life of Sacagawea, the Native Agaidika Shoshone woman who was an unlikely member of the Lewis and Clark Expedition to explore the North American continent.

Sacagawea was taken as a slave when the Shoshone were raided by another tribal nation. She was passed from owner to owner many times; usually, she was lost by her owner when he was gambling. Eventually, she became the property of a Metis, a French Canadian trader; he already owned two other wives.

Sacagawea's life was very hard; however, wherever she went, her character shone through. She was born the daughter of a chief of the Shoshone, and she displayed in her many life roles bravery, industry, intelligence, and resilience.

When Lewis and Clark hired her husband as a translator, they met Sacagawea and recognized her intelligence and her usefulness in dealing with the Shoshone when they went upriver and would have to abandon their canoes and needed horses. Also, as a woman, she brought a feminine aspect to the expedition. She had a capacity to support negotiations that brought peaceful agreements, and through this masterful skill, she became a symbol of peace to the newly forming Nation.

Time and again, Sacagawea proved her usefulness and bravery. Today, this girl/woman (she was just thirteen years old with a newborn when they took her on) is known far and wide for her role in the expedition.

She is such an unlikely heroine to be known about today. She was treated as property, and was oftentimes abused and mistreated, a person of no account. Yet there are places named after her; she is written about, and Sacajawea has become a symbol of the superior virtues of a woman.

There are many who live lives of quiet integrity. Perhaps no books will be written about them; they will not have statues in their image, and they will not have places named after them, yet Sacagawea remains a symbol of the fact that forming a character of good qualities will win out in the end.

When we leave this life, our character, those traits we have built through a lifetime of repeated effort and decision-making, is what we take with us. Our position in life, wealth or lack of it, all of those things that seem so important in this world are all left behind when we leave this body. What we do take with us are those habits that make up our character. In that, we may take inspiration from one small Shoshone woman whose character shone through difficult life experiences and who is known far and wide for the vital role she played in exploring a vast continent.

June 30

NATURE'S HEALING POWER

Glacier National Park, St. Mary's Lake.

I have sought out nature's healing power to support me in recovery after a second major surgery in six months. Even though I live in a beautiful part of the country, there is a draw to going to alpine heights, to deep forests, and to overarching mountains.

Our destination is a place I have not been to before, "The Crown of the Continent," Glacier Park. We have found that it is deserving of its reputation for stunning beauty. Even more to the point, wandering through the woods, hiking along its lakes, and casting an eye on surrounding snow-capped peaks, has brought a palpable healing current from the surrounding nature.

While it is true that spiritual vibration is equally spread throughout creation and we may experience it in any circumstance, it has also been plain that God has wished me to be immersed in Nature's Cathedrals of pristine settings, from desert expanse to lush forest.

I have felt the re-generational force pulsating all around me in our meandering through woods, sitting at the feet of pounding waterfalls, and peering up stark rocked cliffs covered in green, orange, and red lichen.

Nature has indeed come close in the form of a black bear who came visiting at our doorstep. However, the ranger felt it was safer to pepper spray him, of which we got our share of the dosage: making us sneeze, cough, and experience general irritation for some time afterward! I think Mr. Bear definitely felt the welcome mat was rolled up and used to swat him on the head!

One of the interesting points up high is the hydrological apex, one of three in the world. Within inches, a raindrop may land and end up in the Pacific Ocean, the Gulf of Mexico/Atlantic Ocean, or the Hudson Bay/Arctic Ocean. The chance of it landing within inches of this side of the Great Divide or the other, or whether water runs north or south on the east side, makes all the difference as to where that droplet ends up. By chance or by design, depending on your view, it is remarkable to think of the vast differences in destination based on inches of the origin of a plop. It brings to mind the choices we make and where those currents of life take us, based on even a small decision.

Today we took a boat ride up the stunningly aqua-colored St. Mary's Lake. The grinding of the glaciers upon the rock makes "rock flour," a fine rock powder which in turn gives the lake its distinctive and remarkable color. We hiked over three miles to

St. Mary and Virginia Falls, having a picnic lunch in the shade of an 80-degree day. A week ago, I would not have been able to attempt such a walk up and down hills, but today I was satisfyingly tired at its end.

This test of endurance indicates that healing is on a good track. The smell of the trees, wildflowers such as blue lupines, and bright orange/red Indian paintbrush, and the pranic flow of terrific waterfalls bring me strength, inner comfort, and joy. We used the warning bear-bells to accompany our chant of Om Sri Ram, much in the style of the tinkling cymbals of Anandashram, as we moved around blind corners and up and down bear-populated hills.

In short, this rambling narrative is to give you an idea of the physical surroundings and the spiritual vibrancy that has come alive for us here. As I write this, I sit looking out over a meadow that in the distance drastically rises up thousands of feet, where trees give way to steep rock culminating in a peak pointing to the blue heavens. The birds sing, the sun sets behind the opposite mountains, and my heart expands out in universal love—I feel the distinct knowledge that God is sending His blessings to you.

Note: As we drove 30 miles into Browning to get internet to send out this discourse we saw on the smartphone that a young man who worked for the forest service was killed by a grizzly bear while out mountain biking with a friend near the west gate of Glacier National Park. Please say a prayer for him and his family and loved ones.

July 3

SACRED LAND

Divide Mountain: We look out on this mountain
where we are staying. It is considered a very
holy mountain by the Blackfeet Tribe.

Each culture brings unique contributions to the collective
world consciousness. Here at Glacier National Park, we are
in the heart of what had been traditional Blackfeet territory,
to the north was the Kootenai and to the west were the Salish
and Nez Perce.

One of the great strengths of the native population was their
feeling that the land and its animals were sacred. Through oral
traditions, this feeling was instilled in children from a young age.
Taking this single concept, we can all attune ourselves to the
sacred nature of the land we are immersed in.

The emphasis in Western Culture has been to build a house of God—a church, temple, mosque, or cathedral in which God is seen to exist and to be worshipped. One of the things I have written about in particular since going on pilgrimage around North America is finding Nature's Cathedrals—those sacred sites in nature that have existed since its evolutionary beginnings. There are certainly special places that resonate with powerful spiritual vibrations in nature that are systemic to the area itself. Many times, these places will have sacred buildings or associations connected to them created by those who have inner awareness, and then there are times when there is no particular history to a place, but one may feel the spiritual vibrations.

First Nations people certainly had their favored sacred places, but there was also the idea that the earth itself is sacred and that animals play a special role in this interplay between spirit, earth, and humans. Those early inhabitants lived close to the earth's elements, and many were souls sensitively attuned to this connection, open to the transformative experiences that can come by being in untrammeled nature.

As I walk along isolated trails through lush vegetation, there is a vibrancy that shows God is moving throughout all of pristine nature. Birds calling, two bucks lazing next to me as I sit in my chair, a bear visiting at our door, eagles and hawks soaring overhead are all messengers of active spirit moving through its creatures. In this interplay, there is a feeling that there are no accidental movements; these animals are part of an ocean of life-energy. People are not mere interlopers in this creation—but vital parts of it. By being mindful and keenly attuned to the spiritual dimension of creation, new worlds of awareness open to the soul.

The idea of knowing that all creation is spirit is not known by all native people, nor is it barred to others, but the notion is interwoven into traditional culture and the invitation is there for all to become immersed into its deeper mysteries. One needs but a willing heart to go further into this awareness and know that universal Spirit really is all-pervading, including material creation as well as that which is beyond it. No one culture has every aspect of Truth or God in its pocket, but each brings a special view into the limitless variety.

In our time here, in this glacially formed cathedral, we have felt the healing power of nature when walking under its canopy of trees, observing a meadow carpeted with alpine flowers in full bloom and we are open to the many creatures that interplay with us as we visit their homes. We deepen our inner spiritual qualities with the support of Mother Nature's splendors as our souls sing out "Oh God beautiful" in spontaneous response. So, whether it is a walk in your garden, at a local park, or beside a water shore, or observing a mountain view, or passing beside ancient giants of the forest, seek out the healing currents that run abundantly throughout nature and know the great benefits that God is constantly giving to us through this land that is sacred.

Alpine Flowers.

July 6

SUPERIOR INNER NATURE

Looking across the Great Divide to Hidden Lake at the top of the trail.

The power of pristine nature is undeniable. However, it should not be seen in lieu of the power of the life-force that is unleashed in the Son of man, the human form; rather, nature may be seen as an adjunctive help. Spiritual forces within the spine and brain are of unparalleled dimensions.

We celebrated the 4th of July with a traverse up a large snowfield and narrow rocky ledges to the top of Logan's Pass and the crown of the Great Divide. The vistas from the top are spectacular. Mountain goats lazed next to the trail or scampered up vertical rock, beautifully coated marmots drew close, giving us their darshan, and various climbers were festooned in patriotic red, white, and blue. The wind was brisk, and the blue skies and floating white clouds made it a spectacular day.

It seems that I am on an every-other-day schedule: one day exploring nature's wonders, the next indrawn into Spirit's world. Following yesterday's vigorous climb, we are having a quiet day with shorter walks along the shoreline of St. Mary's Lake. We thought of going for another climb today up to a waterfall; however, God had other ideas. According to His whim, powerful currents moved up the spine, making physical activity null and void. With this spinal current heat built up in the cranium, bliss radiated from every cell that made for a deeply indrawn state. Rather than a Ram-adventure in nature, He has orchestrated a Ram-adventure in Spirit.

This life that I lead is a life of complete surrender. God has proved time and again that if something in this world is absolutely required, then He makes it possible for me to do. However, this is not dictated by my preferences or desire nature, but strictly what He wills in any given moment. I am more than happy to surrender to His will, but it supersedes what I think, and sometimes what I think should happen for the sake of others.

This has made for a fascinating life and one that I cannot possibly predict. It has taken me on the most remarkable adventures in Spirit—following in Param-param Gurus' light, He has made me work in ways that defy description. As one who has worked at physical labor since a young age and mental labor years later, this God-work is far more demanding than anything I have known in the world, yet the world would be hard-pressed to recognize it as labor.

There is no doubt that as stupendous as this material creation is—it being far beyond what any of us can know through these five senses—the inner spiritual nature is just that much more. The power of it, the intuitive perception it opens, the satisfaction it provides, the fulfillment of the heart's desires, all of these things make it vastly superior to anything this world, or numberless other worlds beyond, can provide.

An invitation comes directly from the Infinite, "Come, come on this greatest of adventures, the exploration of your own Spiritual Nature." Answering this invitation does require something from you; actually, it requires everything from you. You must be completely dedicated and surrendered to Divine Will.

You may know Divine Will initially as the spiritual practice prescribed for you: meditate morning and night, chant His holy name, practice seeing Him as all in all, be in service to Him in all forms you meet, love Him more than you love the world, and always tell the truth. As you practice these ways with sincerity, an inner life awakens inside of you. Sporadically at first, then continually you know the Divine guidance and Presence through your purified mind—a result of your spiritual practice and Grace.

Now an inner peace and a thrill of joyful bliss permeate your being; you live in total submission to Divine Will expressed through your innermost being. The fullness of this can only be known through direct experience. Do not be left with the regret of wondering why you did not answer God's invitation. Choose it now, today, and every day as you move forward, and you will never look back with regret of any kind. You will then know the superior virtue of your inner nature.

Ascending the ice field.

July 10

Echoes of Infinity

Two Medicine Lake.

Having a guru-lineage in this culture, day, and age is a tremendous boon to all those who have accepted it into their lives. When I met Mother, I had heard of a guru, having read a story of a man meeting his guru, and I had thought, "That is what I need, to meet someone who has gone the way and can show me how to achieve realization."

It seemed a very long time in looking, but in reality, it was less than five months after reading that story when I met Mother. My desire was very strong and the spiritual crisis I found myself in was very deep. Mother was totally unexpected to me, an American woman with a universal message that included strong overtones of the story of Christ. However, her spiritual power and her ability to lift me up whenever I saw her was a wonder and convinced me to my bones that she was my guru.

With time, I discovered the profound meaning of participating in a spiritual lineage. I learned of the ancient and perennial sacred wisdom, first through Mother's stories, and then through her guru lineage writings; that is, her guru Paramhansa Yogananda, her param-guru Sri Yukteswarji, her param-param guru Lahiri Mahasaya, and the heads of this guru lineage—Babaji and Jesus Christ. I was in awe! It took time to slowly assimilate the profound meaning of my relationship with these personages and the legacy of teachings they entrusted to the future. This gift of grace also included the powerful spiritual personalities of Papa Ramdas, Mother Krishnabai, and Swami Satchidananda—there seemed no limit to the spiritual riches that were simply handed to me—to us.

In writing about this now, I melt in gratitude, knowing that I am nothing in the light of these exalted beings. As I melt, I merge in the oceanic bliss of cosmic Spirit. The mind drops to its knees in acknowledgment that it cannot possibly fathom such profundity. To one who has not come into real contact with this kind of relationship, my experiences will simply sound incomprehensible; however, to those who have known a true guru relationship, there is a kindredness of spirit in shared humility and powerful transformation.

When Mother asked me to teach, she taught me to relay my inner experiences to the world. I felt shy in doing so for these experiences are most near and dear to me. It can be painful to relate what is most intimate to one's heart and soul and have it not comprehended or misunderstood. That fear is now long past for me, for I know that those who have eyes to see and ears to hear will find truth in what I say; for others, there is nothing lost because they will go on with their lives none the worse off and I will know joy in finding others, or even just one, who will be inspired by what I say. I know this transformation occurs because I feel the power of truth in me, and I know that truth has the ability to awaken itself in others.

In fact, words are too small to hold my meaning; however, those who receive the spirit that inspires the words will receive both words and spirit and be lifted up into higher regions of thought and spiritual consciousness. When Reverend Bob Raymer first met Master, Sri Yoganandaji repeated the names of the gurus in his ear. Bob was unfamiliar with the sounds of these exotic names and had no idea of what he was saying, but he never forgot the whisper of the master.

I too hear those names whispered into my ear by some mystic means as Master repeats, "Sri Yukteswarji, Lahiri Mahasaya, supreme master Babaji." In those words, I hear the echo of infinity. In saying this, is it madness to think others may hear endless, unfathomable bliss in this ecstatic Reality? Oh, I know there is ground prepared, and even new ground being prepared for these seeds to find rich soil in which shared visions of infinity merge us all into one Reality.

It is in this loving Spirit that I send out on etheric waves the untold blessings that come with inner attunement to our beloved param-para guru-lineage. We are blessed beyond comprehension through our deepened connection with these God-tuned beings—perfected in the fires of testing and blazing with the pure Light of Divine Consciousness.

Health Update: As we have been living in Nature's Cathedrals, this body has grown in strength and endurance. Hikes along lakesides with powerful glacier-cut peaks above, vivid-colored alpine spring flowers at our feet, powerful waterfalls surging and pounding their way in freefall running past us—this has been just what the inner doctor ordered. Thank you for your positive, loving, prayerful thoughts; they truly make a difference. We are now making our way back from Glacier National Park. I highly recommend the experience to anyone who feels the inclination to go. A very happy observation has been the quality of young people working as park rangers. They have been universally positive, informative, and proud to wear the green and gray colors and distinctive hat of a park ranger.

July 13

DARKNESS ABHORS THE LIGHT

Columbia River from Wanapum State Park.

Making our way back from Glacier National Park, we find ourselves next to the Columbia River at Wanapum State Park. In this early morning light, the topic of temptation is uppermost in my thoughts. As we know, temptations are part and parcel of the upward path to realization. Jesus went into the wilderness and was tempted, Buddha sat in his night of temptation just as he was about to attain Nirvana, Rama had times of despair during his struggle to defeat Ravanna and rescue Sita; even these great beings, these avatars, were tempted.

A universal feature of darkness is its abhorrence of the light. What had been perfectly clear to you before, during temptation becomes muddy. Temptation can be of any nature, depending upon the psychological makeup of the individual. It can be sex, drugs, fear, greed, power, pride, self-interest to the exclusion of others, lack of surrender, so many aspects of the opposing force—it will always fight against what the inner soul knows to be true and correct.

The way through temptation is to keep your mind upon God. The qualities you will experience when in tune with God will be quite different from when you are in ignorance. In the light, you will be calm, clear, humble, and not driven by lower forces; you can easily stand in the light in humble submission and not turn away.

One test I would enact for myself when faced with an uncertain decision would be to visualize all the masters surrounding me: Jesus, Babaji, Lahiri Mahasaya, Sri Yukteswarji, Master, Mother, Papa, Mataji, and Swamiji. Then I would present the situation at hand to them. What did they say? I did not avoid any of them as I did this. Many times, when looking at Mother or Sri Yukteswarji, I instantly knew I had been heading into a fool's errand. This worked very well to cut through the mental justifications the ego-mind concocted for going away from the light.

When in Glacier National Park we found a rare hydrological apex, one of three in the world (the other two being in Canada and France). At this apex, drops of rain could land within inches of one another and one would end up in the Pacific Ocean, one in the Atlantic, and the third would be swept off to the Arctic Ocean. So little distance in origin, but such a vast difference in destination. It struck me that choices we make can seem so small and insignificant at the time, and yet forces will sweep us off to such diverse outcomes.

I have known those who were sincere and dedicated to the path, and then some old habit was re-awakened: drugs, alcohol, sex, and the spark of temptation became a flame—the individual was consumed. Or, the spiritual flame was no longer fed with deepened meditation and intense love of God—the flame died and the spark faded to a bygone memory. "Oh, are you still into that?" was the comment, "Yes, I used to be, but now . . . ." The spark that became a flame was now gone, and it seemed but a distant memory.

I know I have had lifetimes of avoiding the light, and in this lifetime, I have made bad choices at times. I vividly remember the pain of those bad choices, both for myself and for others. Through the Grace of God and Guru, the flame did not die; the spark remained even in the looming darkness. It is true, I did choose the light. But better than that, for some unknowable reason, the light chose me and saved me time and again.

There have been those who have thought better of me than I have thought of myself, and this has awakened a higher light in me, made me choose the better path. But we can choose, through pride or arrogance, to push away the light, to respond to those around us that are also pushing away from the light. We have that freedom of choice, but oh what a price we pay for landing on the other side of that decisional hydrological apex!

So, this is the lesson I have come to learn, again and again, the power I have—we all have—in making a choice. Do we choose the light, or do we move into darkness? Do we strive to know God, love God, or do we make choices that ease us away from God just before we find ourselves in a downward plummet away from our higher aspirations? Sri Yukteswar asked Master to promise that he would never avoid him. Master said that was one of the most difficult promises he ever kept in his life. Sri Yukteswarji was the light to Master, and the light can break our pride and crash our dream-desires. Association with the Light will also make us into its own nature—unalloyed peace, joy, and unending freedom—if we only choose it.

July 17

Relations—Attachment and Freedom

Swami Satchidananda: A powerful example of universal love, 2007.

One of the enduring challenges for aspirants comes with the relationships we have in this world, through family, friends, and professions. The fine line of how *to be in this world, but not of it* offers a demanding obstacle course to run, but like all obstacle courses, they are intended to make us better, stronger.

I just attended a birthday celebration for a favorite aunt where I saw cousins and relations I had not seen in years. It was lovely to see these family members who I have known most of my life, exchanging news and whereabouts, catching up on those who were not in attendance, the normal kind of conversations that ensue in such gatherings.

Like the proverbial iceberg, what shows above the surface offers little of what resides below. To be in a group and feel the love and light of the Divine shining through the heart, to embrace each one in that same light is a freeing experience that sheds self-consciousness and makes us see more clearly the real person behind the mask of a social personality.

What prevents this freedom while mingling in the world of relations? It is the set of expectations we hold for ourselves and others, as well as those expectations others hold for us. These expectations are attachments to ideas of who we are supposed to be, or the spoken or unspoken agreement of what others expect of us—keeping us bound to roles that do not reflect who we really are.

"What will others think of me or say about me?" matters a great deal to the ego-mind. "Will they think I have gained a few pounds, lost a few? Will they think I am successful or that I am failing to live up to expectations? Will I be accepted or rejected, embarrassed or proud?" And then there are my judgments of others based on outward appearances. The list of attachments can be very long, all of which keeps me from being present to what is true in the moment. I will fail to see the greater reality when taken in by the outer show; I will be robbed of the greatest gift—universal love.

The truth is we all crave to be loved. However, in the market-place of relationships, we oftentimes only give and receive judg-ments—not love. Of course, we perceive the tip of externals, but do we go beyond *the things of the world?* I alone am responsible for seeing or not seeing higher reality; I cannot expect the world to see it first.

My aunt has the rare quality of seeing the best in others and bringing it out in them. With a twinkle in her eye and a ready laugh—even as dementia is destroying parts of her brain, she retains that which has always been essential to her loving nature.

Life has handed her some very difficult situations, and rather than make her bitter she has compassion readily available for all, as well as righteous anger for those who thoughtlessly heap suffering onto others.

A man recently broke into her room; it had been warm, and she had left the patio door open and fallen asleep. She woke up to a dark room with a strange man reaching to steal her cell phone. Coming out of her sleep, she said, "Get the hell out of here!" She was sure he was more startled than she had been, and he ran from her room. I know that if the man had come back the next day and told her of his difficulties, she would have given him a sympathetic ear, and some stern advice to never do any such thing again.

Someone like my aunt makes it easy to give and receive love. However, others can be more challenging, an obstacle in the course that makes you work harder to remain undisturbed. It is a matter of keeping your mind fixed on your own higher nature. It is common that when you meet someone, you meet like with like. If people are abrasive, invasive, or in some way rub you the wrong way, you feel the need to react to their behavior. You put them in charge by being reactive to how they are presenting, giving them all the power. When you think about it, such personalities would be the last people in the world you would put in charge of your life!

Instead, you exercise self-mastery—focusing on your own higher nature. You continue in your own Light and remain undisturbed by what another says or does. This does not make you a doormat; you may even tell them *to get the hell out!* But you do not lose connection to that vast aspect of yourself that is beneath the surface—your greater qualities.

Practice chanting the all-powerful name of God when in social situations. See the light radiating from your own heart and surrounding those who are around you. Feel the freedom this invokes within you, and you will see it has its effect on others as well. Those who are obstacles to this practice are in your life to make you stronger. Self-mastery teaches you that when you put God first, you will find a peaceful bliss that the world simply cannot give to you—and that universal love will be the hallmark of your life.

July 19

Guru Purnima

Mother Hamilton: Holding
the Light for the world.

In India, Guru Purnima Day occurs on the first full moon after the summer solstice: today. Tonight, I have been gazing up at the full moon as it makes bright the earth below. It is a day to show respect, love, and devotion for one's guru, one's own spiritual teacher, and agent for profound change.

I bow to my Guru, Mother Hamilton, and my guru-lineage. It is due to their selfless service and total dedication that I found the ways and means to attain an illumination that is far greater than either the moon or the sun.

The tradition of Guru Purnima began countless years ago. An unknown yogi appeared in the Himalayas. So many aspirants were magnetically drawn to the sage; however, he appeared as if dead, only tears of ecstasy occasionally ran down his face. Eventually, the crowds left, and only seven remained, determined to get teachings from this obviously great mahatma, this great soul. One day, the yogi opened his eyes, and they asked for his teachings. His mind hovered above dualism and he said nothing. Eventually, through their persistence, they were given teachings tailored to their advancement. They practiced what they were given sincerely, and the silent guru said no more. Years rolled by, decades, and still, the guru made no move. At last, he once again opened his eyes and saw the pure minds those seven yogis had attained through their practice for over 80 years. This Adiyogi, first yogi, was also Adi Guru, first guru, and was none other than Shiva, the Himalayan yogi of extraordinary realization.

The purity of his disciples drew Shiva out of himself and on the first full moon after the longest day of the year, he gave them the cream of his teachings. With those teachings came the understanding that humankind can consciously advance in realization through individual effort—the essence of yoga and all the great religions of the world.

Thus, it is said that the tradition began for honoring one's guru on this most sacred Remembrance Day. I know firsthand the tremendous power that emanates from a fully realized guru. Mother not only gave me the means for completing my realization, but she stood as a protector, guarding me from dark forces.

As I write this, I think of the numberless times that Mother lifted me out of darkness into the Light. On one occasion, Mother saved me from physical and vehicular damage. I was driving to Service on a Sunday morning. I was moving along on Northgate Way when I suddenly saw the car in front of me had come to a full stop. I was driving a van that had no protection in the front.

I locked up my brakes, but I could see that my vehicle was not going to stop in time. I braced for impact. Mother flashed through my mind, then suddenly it was as if a film was spliced—I was twenty feet back from where I previously knew myself to be. I continued skidding, but now I came to a complete rest just inches behind the bumper of the stopped car. What happened, and how it happened, is as deeply mysterious to me today as on that morning; I can only say, "Guru's Grace."

Guru comes in the guise of so many relationships. Mother was teacher, disciplinarian, beloved, confident, psychologist, mystic, pure spiritual power, and light. No other has come anywhere close to changing my life and making it possible for me to make real and meaningful spiritual progress in this life. For that, no amount of words of gratitude can suffice.

Once I said to Mother, "When you leave the body, you should take me and all of us with you; I have no wish to continue if you are not here." She looked at me very sweetly and said, "But who would carry on this work if there were no one left?" So, we carry on in order to do what we can to help her work in the world—the work of lifting this world closer to God. True, there are powerful forces of darkness in operation at this time. However, there are also wonderful souls striving to bring in the Light, for themselves and for this world. Wherever there is courage and dedication to reach out for that Light, then Mother's work will be advanced just that much more. The greatest honor we can pay Mother, Master, and all the guru-lineage is to strive for, and merge into, the eternal light of Being, to bring the bliss of God's presence into our hearts and souls so that heaven and earth may merge and become as one.

Have a blessed Guru Purnima Day.

July 24

Babaji Remembrance Day

Yogacharya David kneels next
to an altar and painting of
Babaji, Dwarahat, India, 2005.**

When I first met Mother, I recognized what a powerful spiritual personality she was. Later, in meeting Swami Satchidanandaji, I experienced his spiritual personality, so different in outward expression than Mother's. Mother came to me as powerful and penetrating, one who could also give the love of a mother. Swamiji was quiet, unassuming, yet commanding the total respect of all those around him. These descriptions are but some of the outward signs of the personalities; however, they both embodied a spiritual presence that defies all description.

And so it happens with all realized Beings—each one has a unique expression. When the personality has been subsumed in Divine Consciousness, if it is the Divine Will, that one is reborn, so to speak, as a Divine personality for the benefit of the world. One of the great lessons you learn in having a pantheon of a guru-lineage and coming into close association with saints is that you do not have to become an imitation of the personality of a God-realized individual; rather, you learn what is essential to all God-realized beings.

And what is essential are the Divine attributes of love, bliss, wisdom, and being a giver of light. In meeting with Mother and accepting her as my Guru, I learned of the great spiritual personalities that make up our guru-lineage. Through Mother's stories and reading the *Autobiography of a Yogi* and other books, I became aware of who these great ones were. However, at first, it was like looking at them through a paned window: there was a view of these enlightened beings, but it was not the same as actually meeting them.

Over the years of discipleship, I had significant experiences that made me know that I had actually touched the fabric of their exalted divine personalities. Lahiri Mahasaya and Babaji were the last two param-para gurus in our lineage that I came into actual contact with—twenty years after meeting Mother. Meeting these great ones was life-changing, right down to the cellular level.

One such incident occurred soon after I had left my work as a counselor/mediator. Phyllis had generously invited me to stay in a little cabin not far from her house on Hornby Island. While on the island, I took walks in Helliwell Park—boasting of magnificent views, old-growth Douglas firs, and rare Garry oaks.

As is my wont at times, I took a late-night walk to a particular place in the park that I had previously felt drawn to. The thought of Babaji came strongly to mind; I knew the great master was making me think of him. An intense desire came into my whole being to be in his presence. I perceived that Babaji was in intimate communion with my mind and a surcharge of spiritual power and realization coursed all through me. As my mind touched his, I was drawn through the woods to the ocean side.

There, I looked up to the canopy of stars, so close that I felt I could reach out to them. The thought came to my mind that Babaji could descend—just as I felt one of those points of light above could come down to earth. Then—I felt enveloped in the great master's presence. The cells of my being were sanctified, as if spiritually baptized through and through. His blessings showered upon me, and I knew that I was touching the hem of Divinity through him. Through direct spiritual connection, I glimpsed his supernal consciousness. Oh, if there were only words to say something of this; however, the words do not, nor can they ever, exist. After some time, the master's presence withdrew, but the afterglow continued as I remained enveloped in his bliss.

Even as we mark Babaji's Remembrance Day (July 25th) and I write of this experience so many years ago now, once again all the cells of my being feel baptized in his holy Presence even as on that sacred night. It is true that we should seek out direct experience in God, without intermediaries. However, how blessed we are to have these great ones actively helping us to that noble Goal of goals. Truly, Babaji, Jesus, Lahiri Mahasaya, Sri Yukteswarji, Master, and Mother all stand at the ready to render us the greatest aid on the most tremendous adventure we will ever embark upon. The Mahavatar is naught else but pure God-consciousness, and thus a direct conduit to the Infinite.

Helliwell Park, Hornby Island, B.C.**

July 28

Ingredients for a Great Marriage

Ralph Hamilton, Papa, Mataji, and
Mother Hamilton, Anandashram, 1957.

One of the great events in life is to be married. However, while the marriage ceremony is not the very start of a relationship—it really is the beginning of a new life together. As a minister, I have the privilege to perform marriage ceremonies, and each joining of a couple brings a special grace that occurs when vows are exchanged. This ceremony is the cradle from which a new-born relationship can evolve—given the right attitudes by the couple.

When standing in front of the couple, a spiritual power transmits itself, and according to the receptivity of each one, the seed is sown. However, the seed must have good ground to land upon in order for it to bear its ultimate fruit. What are the ingredients of that good ground?

Commitment to the ideals of marriage must be the first component in forming a truly successful union. Without commitment, there can be nothing lasting in marriage. The next element must be respect. Unless one shows self-respect and respect for one's spouse, the ground will be spoiled and become inhospitable to growth.

With commitment and respect, the third act must be kindness. Kindness is expressed in thought, word, and deed, and without it the land becomes barren. By tilling the soil with these three essentials, then the fourth essential, love, grows. Love is more than the chemistry of animal attraction or need. Love is the blossoming of the heart that grows and grows, making the soul open to the higher qualities of life. And finally, the fifth element of a truly great marriage is found in Spirit. With the focus on God in the beginning, middle, and end, a marriage rises above simple human fulfillment and becomes something far more. There is a blissful merging of two souls in Spirit—two souls in an ocean of Light. Then, the sense of being two separate identities merges in true union found in God-experience.

In the *Gospel of Swami Ramdas* (October 16, 1957), Mother and her husband Ralph described to Papa what happened when they talked about God with each other. Ralph: "We spend hours together talking about God and losing all count of time." Mother: "We used to talk about God and sometimes we were so much absorbed in Him that our physical bodies would disappear, as it were, and there would be only waves and waves of light between us. This happened many times."

It all starts with how we treat each other day to day. Each soul chooses to incorporate these five elements and makes them part and parcel of how he or she thinks, speaks, and acts in marriage.

Self-respect means you act in a way—that in the end—you will be pleased with and know you have been your best. When you have a spouse who does the same, there are truly no limits to the heights to which two people can rise.

In marriage, you seek to enact Jesus' great saying, "Give, and it will be given to you. A good measure, pressed down, shaken together and running over, will be poured into your lap. For with the measure you use, it will be measured to you" (Luke 6:38). This does not mean that in everything you do you will see like-compensation in every moment. Rather, you build a habit of giving goodness, and it will surely return to you, just as surely as the sun rises in the morning. But most of all, in marriage you give the best of who you are because it brings out the best in you; it is how God-consciousness is made manifest in this world and it is what brings you true and lasting happiness.

July 31

Positive Tapas

Srimad Guru Adi Shankaracharya with disciples
practicing austerities, artwork by Raja Ravi Varma, c. 1904.**

Tapas is an ancient Sanskrit word (tapah) that is translated as austerity (from Latin austerus: severe). It is often thought of as extreme forms of discipline that can extend all the way to self-inflicted torture. However, as Krishna points out in the *Bhagavad Gita*:

> Veneration of the Devas, the twice-born, the gurus, and the wise, straightforwardness, continence, and non-violence are the penance or austerity of the body.

Meditative communion with one's own true Self, and uttering words that cause no agitation and that are truthful, pleasant, and beneficial, are called the austerity of speech. A calm and contented mental clarity, kindliness, silence, self-control, and purity of character constitute the austerity of the mind.

This threefold penance, sattvic in its nature, is practiced by persevering men (and women) possessing great devotion who desire no fruit of actions.[6]

I remember watching a film in a High School class in which some yogis were shown on the banks of the Ganges. Some had kept their arms lifted above their heads for so long that they atrophied in place, and others stared at the sun for so long they were blind. To my mind, it made no sense to do such things. I was not raised Catholic, but I read of aspirants and saints in that tradition where there were similar kinds of self-inflicted tortures on the body in the name of God; this too made little sense.

There has been a long history in all religions of disciplining the body—from fasting and keeping silence all the way to extreme torture. In India, this discipline is referred to as tapasya. While healthy disciplines such as fasting and keeping silence can be aids to the aspirant in rising above this world, the real renunciant goes beyond body disciplines and masters the vacillations of the mind. One may retire to a cave, eschew all but the most basic food, and to all outward appearances be detached, yet the mind continues to crave for things of the world and remains in bondage. On the other hand, one may be surrounded by the things of the world, with responsibilities and varied interests, yet be inwardly detached—such as King Janaka or Rajasi Janakananda (James J. Lynn).

---

6   *God Talks with Arjuna: The Bhagavad Gita* (Chapter 17, verses 14–7).

How to attain a high level of detachment even while living a busy life? One method is to focus on depriving the body in an effort to escape it; however, inwardly the mind can remain focused on what it <u>doesn't</u> want—this feeds the beast rather than frees one from its clutches. In the Gita, Krishna takes a positive approach. Tapas is defined as what to focus the mind on, not what it wants to get rid of, a successful approach that is over five thousand years old.

Krishna lists those things to focus on for the body, speech, and thought in order to free itself from ignorance. For the body, he says to keep your mind on God and His attributes (devas). Devas are either highly evolved beings or aspects of His Supreme Being and are to be worshipped. Others to be respected are your guru and guru-lineage, the twice-born (those who are truly spiritually reborn), and those who display wisdom—all are worthy of your utmost veneration.

In activity, you are simple and straightforward; you are free from lower passions driving your life, and you seek to do that which is only beneficial for yourself and others (non-violence). By working these ways into the field of action in your life, you are practicing penance or austerity of the body.

Practice austerity of speech by saying only that which is true and beneficial. And for your mind, keep calm, clear thoughts that are kind, pure, and established in equanimity. Great devotion to God in body, speech, and mind creates this sattvic (pure, calm) state, which is the basis for Self-realization. Tapas is learning to focus the mind on these positives and giving no power to less worthy thoughts or activities—this is self-mastery.

Through keeping your mind on God and your inner attunement to Him, you may well be prompted to fast, take silence, and not indulge in certain activities in order to purify your body, speech, and mind. However, simply trying to get rid of what bothers you is not enough. There were those who would fast when I did. A

few disregarded the rules for breaking a fast and would raven-
ously eat as soon as they were finished. I had to ask one to stop
fasting, for she would do her body harm by eating large bowls of
ice cream when coming off the fast. Many times, doing something
extreme will have a rebound effect and bring on more difficulties
rather than freedom.

Be determined to be master of yourself, and as a result experience freedom, bliss, and a universal vision. You need not torture
your body in order to do this, even as the Buddha taught the
Middle Way—avoiding extremes. You will find that focusing on
starving the body or trying to make the mind empty without the
uptake of blissful joy and spiritual freedom will not free you.

Meditating upon the great I AM, chanting His name, surrendering to His will, and immersing yourself in the bliss of God
will purge you of every limitation and liberate you in full spiritual realization so that you will never be entrapped in ignorance
again—this is the endgame in the practice of positive tapas. Keep
your mind lovingly focused on God and surrendered to His will; it
is the most positive, easiest, and the most direct way to immerse
yourself in God-experience.

August 3

It Is Either a One or a Zero

Lahiri Mahasaya, when he received word sent by Babaji that the
sands of time were running out for this lifetime, his body
shuddered in reaction, then the great spiritual master immediately
focused on the ajna and merged into Divine Consciousness.

We encounter disappointment, loss, and jolts to our
system on a fairly regular basis on this material plane;
they are, and will always be, part of our lives here. To
weather these storms when they hit us and not allow them to
knock us off balance must be a deep part of our spiritual practice.

The other day, I received some news that was disappointing. I
had been accepted as part of a new therapy in which they took
samples of T cells with the idea that they would grow them in the

laboratory and bank them against a day that I might have more tumors. The cells did not grow; that happens about 50 percent of the time.

Now, news like this can feel like a disappointment in the moment, but how do we keep that from sending us down a spiral into darkness? We have two major parts of our brain—the emotional mind and the reasoning mind. It is primarily the emotional mind that can attach itself to disappointment, loss, or shock and retain it in the body where it loops back to itself in an endless cycle—accomplishing nothing and sinking the emotions into a pool of distress.

We can shift the focus from the emotional mind to the reasoning mind in a number of ways that do not suppress the emotions by denying them, but rather put the reasoning mind in charge to help the emotional mind be useful—not self-destructive.

A way that God gave me to do this was inspired by binary computer coding. A binary code is a series of ones and zeros in different combinations to create a bit string for each symbol or instruction, a mathematical language. The principle for shifting from the emotional mind to the reasoning mind is simple. In life, results or solutions are of two sorts: one is a yes, the other a no; either it is one thing, or it is another. For instance, the results of the lab work with the T cells were either going to be successful in growing the cells, a yes, or it was not going to work, a no. It was going to be a one or a zero.

We can spend an enormous amount of energy worrying about some outcome, but in truth, all the worry in the world does not change what is going to be. Worry also produces a negative result as it stresses our physical and mental health. With the reasoning mind in charge, it can decide on proper action, or to remain in a restful, alert state. The emotional mind drives us to action, but the actions are usually not for the good. Also, the emotional mind acts as static on the mental radio which interferes with the intuition of the Superconscious Mind. So not only does the emotional mind have a negative effect on the body and mind, but it also makes it impossible to hear the still, small voice of God within. The reasoning mind can be employed to become calm in meditation, a perfect receiver for Super-conscious inspiration and guidance. Therefore, the reasoning mind must be in charge.

In anticipating the results of the T cell therapy, I knew it was either going to be a yes or a no, successful growth of T cells or not. In getting the phone call, I thought, "This is going to be a one or a zero, a yes or a no." With a calm mind, I listened to the results, connected with the reasoning mind and the higher thoughts of the Soul.

Even so, when I first heard the results, they came as a dis-appointment; the procedure offered an option for the future if needed; that option is now off the table. As I continued with shift-ing to the reasoning mind and surrendering to God's will, the dis-appointment lifted from me, and the reasoning mind focused on what I could do now. "I do not need these T cells at the moment, and the best alternative is to have no new tumors at all. There are other possible treatments as well; so, let us investigate those to see what is possible." I made three telephone calls to special-ists in the field to alert them to the lab results and to get consul-tations for new options.

The calm mind also focused on the present. I reflect:

> Today, I feel very good. My stamina and general sense of physical well-being are 100 percent; recovery from sur-gery has gone perfectly. God has me busy with His Work. My focus has been on my work for God, and my occa-sional prompting of the medical professionals to ensure they stay on top of my situation. God knows I need more time to complete what I want to finish for Mother's work and my own, and to serve those who are striving for

realization. He knows that my will is surrendered to His will in all matters, but He also knows my preferences.

He also knows your prayers on my behalf—in that I am content. I think of nothing but perfect health; I do all in my power to promote a healthy body, mind, and spirit in all the ways He directs me—in this I am content. God knows the load He has given to me; He gives me the strength to carry it—in this I am content. I live in a human body that has limitations, and He makes me know that I also live in Him, and that has no limitations—and in that, I am also content. In the end, He will decide, moment to moment, what His will is for me, and whether He decides it is a one or a zero—I am content.

August 8

PERFECT FAITH

Jesus Healing the Sick✱✱

We are waiting for news from the latest PET scan from last week. I wrote earlier about shifting from the negative emotions to the reasoning mind (either it is a one or a zero) for making healthy decisions and maintaining a calm mind. The reasoning mind can then meditate and gain access to the inspiring Super-conscious mind.

There is something more than working with the mind in my thoughts today; it is the very interesting role of faith. Jesus said,

"For assuredly, I say to you, if you have faith as a mustard seed, you say to this mountain, 'Move from here to there,' and it will move; and nothing will be impossible for you" (Matthew 17:20). This is a bold thought from the master!

And what does it mean? Surely there are those who claim to have faith, faith in a savior or a deity, but can they move mountains? Jesus must have had a tremendous experience that made him able to make such a fantastic proclamation!

Is faith the power of mind—which is remarkable, but how remarkable is the mind alone? One of the great problems experimental scientists have is accounting for the placebo effect, an effect that is due to the patients' belief that they have been given a treatment, such as a drug, while in fact they have been given a placebo, perhaps only a sugar pill. Patients become well without the "real" treatment; the role of belief is one of the most under-studied effects in medicine. The placebo effect can happen with people from varied backgrounds: those with religious convictions and those without.

But faith is more than mind. Faith connected Jesus with a woman seeking healing in an entirely unconscious way on his part. Out of many in a crowd, Jesus felt the power of God flow through him to one woman:

> And a certain woman, which had an issue of blood twelve years,
>
> And had suffered many things of many physicians, and had spent all that she had, and was nothing bettered, but rather grew worse,
>
> When she had heard of Jesus, came in the press behind, and touched his garment.
>
> For she said, If I may touch but his clothes, I shall be whole.

And straightway the fountain of her blood was dried up; and she felt in her body that she was healed of that plague.

And Jesus, immediately knowing in himself that virtue had gone out of him, turned him about in the press, and said, Who touched my clothes?

And his disciples said unto him, Thou seest the multitude thronging thee, and sayest thou, Who touched me?

And he looked round about to see her that had done this thing.

But the woman fearing and trembling, knowing what was done in her, came and fell down before him, and told him all the truth.

And he said unto her, Daughter, thy faith hath made thee whole; go in peace, and be whole of thy plague.[7]

Time and again Jesus ascribes healings that passed through him to the recipient's faith. Faith—faith the size of a mustard seed, a tiny seed that can grow into a tremendous tree. It is something to think upon, to meditate on. I have meditated on faith many times down through the years and there have been different levels of understanding unfolding before me from its deep mystery.

Belief is something of the mind, but faith comes from some place more fundamental to our being. Faith connects the mind, in a viable way, to the supreme power of the Creator and in that connection, the higher power of Grace flows. The direction in which Grace goes can be interactive; we may direct that power through our intention, such as when we pray for another, or the inner power will also direct us, as when virtue goes out of us spontaneously.

---

7   Mark 5:25–34.

Faith is not simply desire or belief; it is true contact with God. Such contact requires not only Grace on Spirit's side, but purification on the human side. Once when Jesus' disciples were unable to cast out lunacy in a man's son, Jesus pointed out their failure was due to the disciple's unbelief; the kind of faith needed for this particular situation required preparation and purification through fasting and prayer.

Through deeper meditation, the aspirant achieves true God-contact: a knowing connection grows and convinces the devotee down to the cellular level that God is with him or her. When the power of God passes through that devotee, then healing of the body, mind, and spirit occurs; also, courage, clarity of mind and purpose, and joyful bliss can be transmitted. With a clear connection to God, mountainous obstacles are removed—and if God wills it, physical mountains tumble down as well.

Attunement to God's will makes all actions taken by the devotee for the highest good of all. There are times when change does not come, even if it is wanted by the disciple. Not everyone who came to Jesus was healed, and even in his own life, Jesus asked if the cup of crucifixion might be taken away, but in the greatest moment of surrender, the master said, "Not my will, but thine, be done" (Luke 22:42). There are times when the drama must unfold; that will be for the highest good of all.

This morning, all these thoughts about faith are passing through me while I wait on the results that will determine the next phase of life for this body. My faith is that all that is unfolding is for the highest good of all. I know that my part is to perceive only perfect health: in body, mind, and spirit. In my touching the fabric of God's Being, I feel peace. I feel the love and prayers you send me, that join you to me and me to you, and in that love, I feel my infinite Beloved. Thus, riches stream to me, and this very moment is perfect.

Thank You, O Lord, for Your virtue flows to all, bringing Your perfection to all receptive hearts. Bless Your children with perfect faith, ever in God Christ Gurus.

August 12

JOY IN VICTORY

Krishna Shows Arjuna His Universal Form: Arjuna is granted
the universal vision in which he sees all, both edifying
and terrifying as expressions of the One perfect God.**

ealth Update: Today we received the results from the PET
scan done last week. Good news, the scans were clean:
no sign of tumors. Thank you for all of your loving support and prayers; it makes the difference. The news brings great
joy. We discussed options with the oncologist for treatment
going forward. A viable option is to begin a series of immunotherapy infusions. There will be more consultations as we go forward—for today, we feel pleased with the results.

The joy that I feel has led me to reflect on the role that being either pleased or disappointed plays in our lives. For pleasure ever alternates with painful situations that occur in life as well. Going back and forth between joy and sorrow is the plight of the human condition. In the Gita, Krishna points out that this alternation binds us in ignorance. Why is this ignorance? Because we identify with the body through our attachment and attraction to joy, to repulsion, and to sorrow. This attachment is never-ending and breeds the delusion that "I am happy or sad" based on momentary situations.

Attachment works in both directions. We can be equally attached to joy and pleasure, as well as sorrow and pain. It is one of the great mysteries as to how or why we would be attached to pain, but many are. In fact, we can tell by what people talk about and what they emphasize as to what their attachments may be. For many, it is the misery in life that captures and keeps their attention. However, we cannot have sorrow without joy, nor can we have pleasure without pain. Great attraction for one side and being repulsed by the other is the source of our attachment.

Applying the principle of detachment to my current situation is a great field-test. This latest scan has vital implications for the health of this body, so approaching the test and waiting for the results have kept it all in my mind. But what has been even more prominent during this time is the work I have been doing on the diary that Mother's husband, Ralph, kept when they traveled around the United States in 1954. As I typed out the handwritten notes, it felt as if I were traveling with them. It was during this trip that Mother worked to shore up the Self-Realization Fellowship (SRF) Centers around the country after Master's passing. It was also on this journey that she entered into Nirvikalpa Samadhi for eleven days, receiving revelations while in this rare and exalted state. Ralph's diary is interesting on a human level and also because of the hints it gives of the spiritual glory Mother was experiencing at the time. So, even though I had to keep track of appointment dates for my tests, my mind was taken up with the spiritual life of my Guru.

When we practice detachment, does that mean we live a life empty of pleasure and pain? This cannot be, for this world of duality cannot exist without them. The news that brings us smiles will one day turn into news that is displeasing. We ride the wave of happiness only to get crushed in the swell of sorrow.

How do we get out of this endless cycle of highs and lows? Only by attaching ourselves to something superior, higher, and more enlightened can we free ourselves from lowly passions and attachments. First, we learn to discern what is higher from what is lower. By letting go of lower passions, and striving for what is uplifting, we enter into an inner stillness. It is this stillness that connects us to pure Divine Consciousness—and through identification with God-consciousness, we transcend life's highs and lows. This realm of pure Being brings about peace and an inner knowing that we are more than the body, emotions, and thoughts—we are no longer ruled by them.

We continue to live life, we feel the waves of joy in accomplishment, we may feel sorrow at a loss, but being anchored in the Divine, we never lose connection with who and what we truly are. We experience ourselves to be the vast ocean of consciousness underneath the ever-changing waves—the alternations of being happy and sad only play on the surface, never touching our deeper Self. For the aspirant who has a purified mind, this is salvation. By knowing our true Self, we cast off delusion's net and free ourselves from the endless cycle of gain and loss. Now we know ourselves as the ever-blissful ocean of God-consciousness.

While waiting for the results of this latest scan, I was busy with God's Work, feeling His Bliss and Power pouring through this little human frame. And with a focus on today, I take joy in the freedom of having a clean scan, and I am happy to share that wave of joy with you.

August 14

YOUR TEMPLE-HOME

Reverend Jill and Greg in their new Temple Home.

Today we have celebrated a House Blessing for Jill and Greg. The blessing took me back in time to when the seed of a thought to do House Blessings first came to mind. It was in 1999 at Anandashram when I was invited to the room of a couple who worked in the ashram and were moving into their new quarters. Swami Satchidananda was the honored guest, incense was lit, and the group rang out with Ram Nam for some time, then Prasad (blessed food) was served to all participants.

I thought, "How wonderful to start out your new home with blessings of enlightened souls and the sacred chanting of Ram Nam." In India, the center of daily spiritual life is not the temple, but is right in the home. Devotees set aside a room, if they have the space, or a part of a room for puja—a dedicated space for devotion to God. Temples are generally used for special occasions and as pilgrimage spots, but regular worship of God occurs in the home. This spiritual center becomes the nexus of blessings for the entire family and community through devotee God-contact. Where better to strive for realization than in your own home?

To dedicate the home to being a Temple-home is the intention behind the House Blessing. A spiritual atmosphere is built with chanting, prayer, and meditation by all who attend. This jump-starts the higher vibration that is then continued by the regular practice by the householders. The spiritual atmosphere seeps into all activities of the home, both sacred and mundane. The power of Divine Consciousness is a blessing to the household, the community, and, if we would but know it, an unlimited potential for how far those uplifting vibrations can radiate from sincere practitioners.

This all-in-one package of the Temple-home supports the family in so many ways. When purity pervades the atmosphere of a home, a natural filter is created that makes bad behavior feel doubly inappropriate; it just feels out of place. On the other hand, spiritual power makes doing what is right and uplifting natural. This power also extends itself to the community in which the Temple-home resides, thus benefiting so many with or without their awareness. In an intentional experiment, a meditation group meeting once a week saw a significant reduction of crime according to police statistics in a rough part of town after they began their weekly one-hour meditation.

It truly is a great thing when you dedicate a space to your practice. It may be a room, a corner of a room, or a closet space you claim. Your practice builds a power in that space, just as it does in the things you use, such as your meditation blanket, beads, and altar. If, on one of those days, you feel drained or uninspired, the vibration you have invested into your meditation space will lift you up and support you—helping to transform a tough day into a good one.

Gradually, the walls, floors, everything in your room and home resonates with that higher vibration and others who enter your home will feel it as well. Even those who are not attuned to spiritual practice will comment that your home feels peaceful, or they just feel good when they enter in; in some notable ways, they will recognize there is something differently salubrious about your home.

You start by feeling peace and upliftment, making God contact during your practice. Then you can consciously radiate that experience out to your home, community, the world, and creation itself. In feeling the vibrancy in the room, your room then becomes transparent and the power you feel goes out and out as your consciousness expands with this feeling. God Himself is working through you to bless this world. There is nothing greater in this world than to be a conscious instrument in the hands of the Divine. You and all those sincere in their spiritual practice invisibly unite to lift this world up for much-needed harmony, peace, light, and love. In this way, your Temple-home becomes a blessing for one and for all.

August 21

Don't Eat, God First!

Holding the World in our hands.**

We have had the joy of hosting some special souls this last week, four growing boys. The energy, the inquisitive minds, and the underlying spirituality are a wonder to see. They hold the future in their hands. With the beautiful souls I have seen coming into Kriyaban households, I feel that the future will bear bright lights to help this world become better—with increasing Light.

Each generation has its own challenges. When I was growing up, there was the threat of a nuclear holocaust that would destroy the world as we knew it looming over us. Here in America, prosperity grew, but a war in Vietnam became extremely distasteful. It was a younger generation in which many challenged accepted norms and were bent on experimentation. Like all experiments, there were many misfires, some of which we continue to live with today. Drugs, sex without restraint, and in some cases a total lack of personal responsibility, are the dregs we continue to see. On the other hand, racial equality, concern for the environment, and a desire for the betterment of all people have grown through that same time frame.

Many times, the real impact of a time period cannot truly be evaluated until many generations have passed. There are some obvious hallmarks of our time: travel to the moon, technological growth, producing food for seven and a half billion people (in the 1970s, this was thought impossible), and a general peace around the world (if one compares today with the World Wars and conflicts of the 20th Century).

What will the future bring? Will computer modeling be correct about a global warming disaster? Will there be new devastating wars or major acts of terrorism? Will irresponsibility and greed lead to economic catastrophe? On the other hand, will international cooperation and competition create a more prosperous world with cleaner air and water? A safer world?

New generations will collectively help determine the answers to these questions. Sri Yukteswarji said that we are emerging from dark ages into greater light. Mother Hamilton added that the age of darkness we are coming out of was an unusually dark cycle from which it has been very difficult to emerge. The challenges are great, but the possibilities are even greater. Great souls can help lift this world into a new age of world peace and enlightenment.

There are indeed high souls incarnating, offering hope not only for material prosperity, but also for greater peace and harmonious living with nature. However, most importantly, first offering the basic foundation that makes all those great things sustainable going into the future—spiritual progress, both individually and collectively. Hope looms, as reflected in what little five-year-old Aron said when we sat down for our meal this last week, "Don't eat, God first!"

August 24

MY CUP RUNNETH OVER

My Cup Runneth Over (Psalm 23:5).**

The conscious mind is a cup that holds the content of whatever your attention is focused upon. When the body demands your attention, the mind naturally is full of worldly concerns. When those concerns make you think that you are either gaining or losing something, then craving, dread, and unrest fill the cup. For many, their cups are filled to the brim with the things of the world.

When you want to focus on God-experience and the cup of your mind is already filled with worldly concerns, then where is there room? In order to know God, you first empty your cup of the things of the world; only then do you have the room needed for contact with the Infinite.

"Be still, and know that I am God" is your goal. Being still is not just sitting quietly; it requires that you empty the cup of your mind of all material concerns. You do this by shifting your attention to God-consciousness.

Being aware of your breath—you feel His peace. Thinking on God's name at the Christ Center—His light fills your Being. Going within—you inwardly hear His all-powerful voice as the Aum/Amen. Through expanding consciousness—you experience His bliss. Your cup is sanctified, no longer polluted with fear, greed, and jealousy. You cannot hold it all and your *cup runneth over*—bliss, light, and the power of the Infinite pour out of your cup, flowing out in blessings to one and to all. Now the cup of your mind is completely still—His blissful Presence fills you without end.

August 28

DECISIONS

Himalaya Highways: Bus on a mountain road in India.**

D ecision-making goes right to the heart of how we live our lives. From deciding what to eat to whether we buy a new car or house, or making a business or professional decision—decisions are an important part of everyone's life.

Being an aspirant for realization means that decision-making may look different to you than to others. If your spiritual life does not inform you about the way you make decisions, then it has not penetrated deeply enough into your life. For some, simply making the decision to meditate daily and attending Center meetings may feel enough. But once you enter into your everyday life, there may be little carryover; you suddenly revert to habits that may or may not serve you. It bears examination to observe how your spiritual life moves into the most basic ways you live.

First of all, you create the intention that every part of your life—what you do, what you think—will be in concert with the spiritual principles you believe in; this congruity keeps you from hypocrisy. Whether it be home life, business, profession, leisure time, or poking around on websites, are you in keeping with your higher ideals? When you make a decision to purchase something, do you do it from a calm, centered state of being?

It is in that calm state of mind that you take the next step in decision-making. Smart decisions require that you gather what pertinent information you can before proceeding to make a choice. So many poor decisions come about from not thinking through the consequences, or not taking the time to consult with those who have seasoned experience with what you are doing. Such information gathering will help you avoid many mistakes others have made and thereby make the right choice.

My father had a very ugly grandfather's clock that he kept in his study for several years. When I asked about it, he said he had ordered it by phone, thinking the advertising was accurate, and he did something very rare for him, he made a snap, impulsive decision. When he received the large clock, he of course immediately saw what a huge mistake he had made. The reason he kept the clock sitting in front of his desk, instead of consigning it to a funeral pyre as it deserved, was to remind him never to repeat that mistake again!

After gathering adequate information, then reason it through. Some people add up the pluses and minuses of a decision on paper, while others reason it out in their head or talk it out with others. Is this decision right for you, as well as for those the decision affects? Are you calm, centered? Or are you acting out of pure desire nature, impulsiveness, fear, or greed? No good can come from the latter, even if it happens to be the right move, because you have not been in concert with your higher nature. One method I have used for making bigger decisions is giving it the "24-hour rule." Wait 24 hours before you make a final decision. It is amazing how clarifying a one-day cycle can be.

Finally, what distinguishes "the men from the boys," spiritually speaking, is giving the whole decision to God. This takes discipline, a calm-centered mind, and surrender. When you have gathered information and reasoned it through, then in your mind, surrender it all to God. You pray: "Lord, make this be for the highest good of all." When you have given it to God, then listen quietly within. Do you feel a green light, go ahead at full speed? Or do you sense a yellow light, proceed with caution? Or do you have a red light, stop right here and now? If inner direction makes all of your plans and anticipations suddenly come to a complete stop, it can really test your resolution to give it to God. Perhaps you feel something is being taken away from you in that moment.

I met a man who ran an internet café in India. When I told him I was traveling in India on a pilgrimage, he shared two incidents from his life. It was obvious he did not regularly think about God, but he had some fascinating experiences. When he, his father, and an uncle were coming down from the mountains by bus, they had left early and paid extra money to take the express bus. This bus made few stops and arrived hours earlier than the second bus, what we would call the "milk run" bus. The second bus stopped for anyone who waved it down, even if that person was still high up on the mountain and far away from the bus.

When they stopped at one of their few scheduled places, they stood around the bus taking in some fresh air before they boarded again. A swami who had been riding on the bus approached the uncle and told him that the three of them should wait for the "milk run" bus and not proceed on the express. This man's father was not in favor of listening to the swami, but the uncle said they should not ignore his advice. So, they waited for the follow-up bus as the father quietly fumed.

Finally, the second bus came, and they boarded. As they made their way down the curving mountain roads, only as roads can curve in the mountains of India, they came to a group of people standing on the road. The bus stopped and all got out to see where the express bus had plunged hundreds of feet down after missing the curve. The uncle asked the swami why he had selected only them to get off the bus. The swami said he saw the mark of death on everyone on the express bus except the three of them. They turned to look down at what would have been their certain fate had it not been for the swami's intervention and were deeply disturbed, yet felt very blessed. When they turned to thank the swami, he was nowhere to be found. The mystery deepened when they asked others from the bus where the orange-clad swami had gone. Every one of them said they had not seen any swami on the bus.

Thus, God can seemingly interfere with all your well-made plans, but what of it! Is He not the loving hand behind everything that happens in His devotee's life? When He tells us to get off the express bus, we are so happy to travel on; we are best served by listening to Him.

August 31

The Art of Balance

Balance is the key to life.**

For the spiritual aspirant to find balance in this world is a great art. Everyone who inhabits a body by necessity has to live in this world. It is an interesting paradox that many who renounce this world and become swamis, monks, or priests can end up running large spiritual institutions, with more organizational responsibilities than an ordinary householder would ever have. You cannot escape this world, even if your only possessions consist of a begging bowl and a water pot.

The art of attaining balance has to be found within, so that even if you are King Janaka with incredible wealth and power, surrounded by all the beauty in this world, you could let it all go up in smoke if God has you otherwise occupied with doing His work. It is impossible to know by lifestyle who has attachments—a person with very little in this world may be more attached to what they have than one who has remarkable wealth and possessions.

My mother-in-law spoke a few times about a family that was torn apart after the death of the adult-children's parents. She said that some did not talk to each other after that, even though the things they were arguing about were "just junk." I knew someone who said goodbye to a long-term friendship after a dispute over a cheap lawn chair. Attachment can bind us to the most inconsequential things.

Yoga means to yoke ourselves to God, not this world. Yet, we are expected to be good stewards of what God has given us. At one time in her life, the only thing Carla had of value was a not-so-fancy car, but she made sure that she washed and vacuumed it so that it always looked its best. We work to find that balance so that we take good care of the things we are given, whether it be a few humble things, the responsibilities of a job or profession, or the ownership of a large company with many employees.

And with mindfully caring for things you have been given, you work to bind yourself to God-consciousness, making that your primary relationship in life. In doing so, you can expect to have freedom from anxiousness, to feel peace in the midst of activity; you will intuitively know that the decisions you make are for the higher good of all, and you will fulfill the purpose for which you have taken incarnation.

To practice detachment, you can think about "what ifs." What if God directed you to walk out your door and leave your home behind? What if He took away cars, furniture, bank accounts? Obviously, you would need a place to live, food to eat, and clothes to cover you, but what if He took away all that you now have? If you are like me, you may have some sense of relief, "Now that responsibility is gone."

I love the home God has given us, the vehicles, furniture, and all the rest of it. I have great gratitude for Carla's and my parents for gifting us with these wonderful things; that we can do the masters' work here and share it with all of you brings about its most significant meaning to me. When I think back to the time when God asked me to enter into this journey without the "safety net" of a paying job, it was quite a mystery to me how God would provide. I had no fear that He would, only how would He do it? And do it He has, with great aplomb!

But just as He has given, so will He take away; even at the moment of death, the great equalizer, when all that any one of us takes with him or her is the innermost self. If, in that moment of separation from the body, you are unfamiliar with your true Self, the part of you who knows God, then you will naturally look to leaving this world with fear and attachment—this attachment is what compels you back into material existence again and again.

Only when you have the balance to walk out of the doorway of this body without attachment are you truly free to explore the vast infinite reaches of Divine Consciousness without fetter or limit—you are then a jivanmukta, a truly free soul.

September 4

SOMETHING BEAUTIFUL FOR GOD

Mother Hamilton and Mother Teresa, Calcutta, 1977.

Today, Mother Teresa of Calcutta officially becomes "Saint Teresa" of Calcutta. The Catholic Church has a formal process of canonizing an individual as a saint: it incorporates at least two verified miracles after his or her death when he or she has prayed for intercession. The real hallmark of a saint, we feel, is that they have led a life surrendered to God—that a saint knows God.

One of the interesting things about Mother Teresa was her inner life with God that was known only to a very few during her lifetime. After receiving a tremendous experience in God that set her out on her mission to serve the poorest of the poor, Mother

Teresa did not experience God's Presence. Not only did she live alongside the poor in Calcutta, but she also lived a life of spiritual impoverishment. In this way, she was meant to serve the poorest of the poor through her example of living simply, and struggling spiritually, while in total surrender to God.

Who could look at her life with an honest view, and not find absolute surrender to her Lord in what she accomplished? I have read her critics, but found no real basis for doubting her sincerity and holiness. Even as she lived, Mother Teresa was a saint. Anyone who takes on a greater mission in life will have oppositional forces to deal with; that will be a certainty. And it is not that we should simply accept easily someone's sincerity and lack of hypocrisy; however, we should not lack faith that there are those, even those in the international spotlight, who can rise up to sainthood.

Saint Teresa of Calcutta stands as a world-wide symbol today of service to the poor—a service in surrender to God's will. Mother Hamilton, in a Christmas talk in 1980, spoke of Saint Teresa after meeting her in Calcutta, and this is what she said:

> The real meaning of Christmas is giving, to give to the poor, to give to the needy, to serve the Christ in every man even as Mother Teresa does in Calcutta, India. She is a world-famous Christian saint and, certainly, she shouldn't have to wait until after she has died to be canonized because she is a saint now. I have but to close my eyes, and I see this woman's face before me—not beautiful in the human sense, in the ordinary physical sense at all—her face is lined with wrinkles; her features aren't too good. But she has a light blazing in her eyes and a light on her skin such as I have never seen before. It is beautiful. And she takes the lepers; she goes out and picks up the

sick and the dying off the streets, and she takes them home to her hospital. And she washes them with her own hands and makes them clean, and she puts clean garments on them, and she teaches these people about the Christ. And each one that comes before her is her Christ in human form. Now, this woman is a great, great Christian, believe me, she is great. She really serves. She is completely without thought of herself. She thinks only of God through Christ and of serving him in every waking moment of her life. She gets very, very little sleep. She works ceaselessly. She uses everything that is given to her in order that she may serve her Christ, and her name has spread all over the earth. Still, when she was given the Nobel Prize and they asked her if she had any comments to make about it, she said that all the honor that had been paid to her was nothing more nor less than crucifixion. She had to take time out to come and appear before a world audience to accept an honor which she gave only to Christ, and so she felt that that was crucifixion. That is true humility, isn't it? And if each of us could be humble in that sense, if each of us, each moment of the day, not just at the Christmas season, but beginning this moment, would look for people to serve, to serve Christ in them, even until you die serving Christ, what more glorious end could you have?

And I will close with a quote from Saint Teresa taken from a book about her entitled, *Something Beautiful for God*.

That's the spirit of our society, that total surrender, loving trust and cheerfulness. We must be able to radiate the joy of Christ, express it in our actions. If our actions are just useful actions that give no joy to people, our poor people would never be able to rise up to the call which we want them to hear, the call to come closer to God.

—Mother Teresa

September 9

THE INWARD MIND

Yogacharya David: Indrawn mood, Anandashram, 2007.

earning to draw our attention to the inner mind is a most wonderful and beneficial practice. It is only when we can turn within that we may contact God. At first, it is difficult because the mind is unruly and is not used to being quiet, but with practice, we learn the wonders that are residing right inside of us.

It is the early morning hours today, and I am drawn to sit in a half-lotus posture. I am sitting straight; a few micro-adjustments in the spine and neck occur along with a few pops and cracks. Spontaneously, the ajna, the point between the eyebrows, acts as a magnet, drawing to it my attention and life-energy. My body is set, my mind turned within.

An intense blissful feeling comes into my spine. It is not specific to the spine only, but radiates out through all the body cells. The voice of God, resounding as the holy Aum/Amen, is heard through the inner ear, bringing a feeling of pressure at the back of my head. Just as the blissful feeling is not distinct to my spine only, so does the Aum/Amen expand out and out. This is a quality of spirit; it can be specific to a location, and it is also part of all-space; it can be as tiny as an atom or bigger than the universe—and it can be so simultaneously.

Then the Light of God lights itself in the ajna. Initially, I see it as a bright star, then it illuminates the cranial cavity in a luminescent glow. Again, it defies being in a defined space, rather as the attention expands, so does the light. Awareness and light, awareness and sound, awareness and bliss merge and all are one—as awareness grows, so does the light, sound, and feeling of bliss, and those qualities of God-consciousness focus or expand my awareness in whatever way they will, and in all of this I am surrendered to what experience He chooses for me.

This experience is vastly superior to all sensory stimulations. It feels like home, and it makes a home of wherever I find myself. The intelligence and wisdom of God play through my mind. All consciousness is instantly accessible. The thought that Lahiri Mahasaya's Mahasamadhi and birthday are coming up at the end of this month flows through my awareness, and with it, a feeling of warmth and love sweeps over me.

Then I feel the master's mind transfer a thought into my own: I should make a diary note of my inner experiences today and make it a post. I submit to his request knowing that he will express what he wants through my receptivity. Lahiri Baba wants us to know that even with the great gift of Kriya and all the writings about the spiritual journey, the inner conscious contact with the supreme Being is simplicity itself. We should practice faithfully,

but not become overly focused on all the complexity of techniques and teachings—only go directly to the Source.

With this thought, a blissful surge goes up my spine and I have
a tremendous feeling of pervasive peace. God is here, God is now.
You only need to keep with your practice, remain receptive, and
the yeast of the God-seed within you will find the right conditions
to grow, flower, bear fruit and ripen into full God-experience. It
is not far away or in some distant time, but within easy range of
your inward mind.

September 12

Happy Journeys Powered by Aum

Double rainbow along the roadside.**

We are on our way to see some of Nature's Cathedrals, driving long hours and enjoying seeing new scenery along the way. Driving is something most all of us do: commuting to work, running errands, taking trips, or doing it for a living.

Our modern way of living means that many of us spend hours a day behind the wheel. Now, for some, driving comes naturally, while others feel anxious. Is there something our spiritual practice can add to our comfort and efficiency while driving for both the natural and the nervous?

The answer is yes, and breathing is the first place to start. The importance of breath was discovered by yogis thousands of years ago, and whether it was shared knowledge or something found independently is, as of yet, unknown. Ancient Judaism also recognized the essential nature of the breath—often referring to it as "the wind" in the scriptures.

Breath is king, and when the air we breathe and the life-force are properly understood, it can control the body-mind-spirit connection. When driving, it is essential to breathe into the stomach, making the diaphragm work up and down—the stomach cavity rising and falling with each breath. In your mind's eye, see the life-energy around your neck and shoulders "breathing" with you, expanding and contracting with each breath. This will relax your body: shoulders and neck relaxed, jaw and arms releasing tension, keeping you relaxed and alert. It is amazing how much energy we burn up with tension in the muscles because the mind and breath are tightened.

Along with breathing, keep your attention at the ajna and mentally repeat Hong-Sau or Ram Nam. As long as you are comfortable with driving and keeping a part of your mind on God through mantra, it will attune body, mind, and spirit into one homogeneous being. I very rarely listen to the radio, music, or even talk when driving. I am very entertained, hours-long, by God. Mile by mile goes by as I feel the Aum/Amen power at the back of my head and vehicle and experience His thoughts flowing through my mind. I do not have a bumper sticker, but if I did, it would read, "Powered by Aum!"

Master's twenty-point recharging exercise is wonderful for relaxing and recharging your body on long trips. Simply tensing and releasing each muscle group and feeling the life-energy flowing is both soothing and awakening to your whole body while driving long stretches of straight road.

Also using the palms of your hands can help soothe and re-energize your eyes. If comfortable for you to do, rub your hands together to charge them with life-energy (otherwise, just put your palm to the eye). Then, using one hand at a time, hold it up to your eye and cover it with the palm of your hand. This will feel warm to your eye and will rest and recharge that eye; hold it for as long as it is comfortable. Then raise the other palm to the eye. This is wonderful when you are driving at night and the lights of oncoming cars tire your eyes.

These yoga practices are pragmatically useful for driving, taking the stress out of it for you, re-energizing your body when fatigued, and attuning your entire self with God. Truly, driving can be a wonderful meditation. You will need to experiment to see what you are comfortable doing, but any or all of these methods will greatly benefit you during the time you spend behind the wheel. Blessings to you and happy journeys.

September 15

BADLANDS ARE NOT SO BAD

Black Hills in South Dakota, middle hill
turns black as cloud passes overhead.

We have discovered the natural beauty of the Black Hills in South Dakota. The Badlands in the Black Hills were so named by the French trappers who were the early European explorers of the area and found it without water, sun-baked in the summer, and very cold in the winter.

Wandering through these hills, we found nothing bad in them, but we do have the luxury of water, modern conveyance, and we are here in temperate September. Lessons abound in nature that relate to our spiritual journey and with a listening mind, we come away much the richer.

The Black Hills received their name due to the fact that the white-colored landscape turns black when the clouds pass overhead, making a stark contrast of white-and-black-colored hills. This reminds us that Spirit, being the sun, and the white hills, being the purity of creation, can appear black when the clouds of ignorance, maya, pass between the pure sun and creation below. In truth, creation has always been pure, only the clouds/maya make it appear dark and black. Remove the veil of maya (the clouds) and all of Spirit and creation are once again seen in their innate purity.

Another desert lesson comes from a beautiful flowering plant that is growing out of an impossible sunbaked clay ground. How can it be that such a glorious plant exists with such harsh conditions above and below? The take-away lesson: beauty can grow in the most terrible conditions. In fact, the reason this plant stands out is that its situation is so forbidding.

Wildflowers.

We stand atop a pinnacle and all around are ravines and rugged landscape where wind and water have sculpted dramatic pointed peaks and sharp drop-offs. The feeling here is purity itself. One of the lessons in going to Nature's Cathedrals is that there is a difference between the visual beauty of a place and its spiritual ambiance.

A feeling of great purity in the Black Hills.

There are places where I have seen a magnificent view, then in some little out-of-the-way spot I suddenly feel God's Presence. It reminds me of some of the great man-made Cathedrals: the main sanctuary may be beautiful and is the center of attention, but then I find a little chapel off to the side and I am lifted up in Spirit. The power of the Presence in that unanticipated location is intimately connected. Lesson: be always attentive to God's Presence; you can never guess when or where it will take you up.

Always, as I merge into Spirit in these holy places, I also feel my connection with all creation—with you, my friends. There is something endemic about Spirit that naturally shares itself with all, whether that be residing in Spirit, through service, or by posting these words—God shares. And in that spirit, my heart goes out to you as we continue to seek out Nature's Cathedrals.

September 18

FROM WALL DRUG TO MT. RUSHMORE

Impressive Mt. Rushmore.

As part of our tour to Nature's Cathedrals, we have had a few "tourist stops" along the way. One is a most peculiar destination. Anyone who has traveled on the highways of South Dakota has surely seen at least dozens of the many thousands of billboards measuring the miles to a tourist attraction called Wall Drug.

I drove through South Dakota many years ago on business and remembered seeing the signs and could not imagine what would warrant such publicity. However, I drove right on past not bothering to find out, but the wondering-thought has been in my mind for these many years. God has a way of fulfilling even our smallest wish, if you could even call this a wish!

Coming out of the Black Hills and the Badlands National Park, our road took us straight to Wall, and of course, we just had to stop in to answer that long-ago question that had stubbornly lodged itself in my mind (we have to be very careful what we allow into our minds!). Well, the story of how this drugstore in Wall became so famous that there are advertisements as far-flung as Paris, France, and Australia is really quite amazing.

Our story begins with Ted and Dorothy Hustead. Ted graduated and worked as a druggist for a few years before striking out on his own. He took a small legacy and bought a drugstore in the town of Wall. In deciding to settle in Wall, Ted's first priority was to live in a place where there was a Catholic Church so he and his wife could attend Mass every morning. The priest, doctor, and banker all assured the Husteads that Wall "was a good place with good people."

The year was 1931. Wall was a town of only 326 people and Ted's cousin ruefully told them that the town was in the middle of nowhere and everyone was flat broke. Even Ted's father-in-law told him that Wall was just about as Godforsaken as you can get. In the end, though, everyone felt that it was God's will for them to move there. Then the testing began. Business was bad and didn't improve. Dorothy said she was sure their abilities could be used in Wall; Ted said he would give it five years for the business to work.

They weren't starving and they made good friends, but whole days went by when Ted was staring out from the store's front door. Flash-forward, with just months to go in their five-year plan, the business had not grown, and they were much discouraged. They had two children to consider, and the future looked bleak.

One hot summer afternoon, Ted was busy swatting flies with a rolled-up newspaper and looking out on a street with no traffic. Taking a rest with her baby, Dorothy came up with an idea. Route 16A passed the town by with traffic that had no reason to stop.

Dorothy had a flash: put a sign out for free ice water in the sweltering heat (remember this was before cars had air conditioning). They put the sign out on the highway and the cars and people didn't stop coming, and of course, they would pick up a few items at the drugstore while getting free cold water and coffee for a nickel.

Very soon, they had eight young women employees selling ice cream cones and sundry. Today, they have over a million visitors a year, and twenty thousand customers on any particular scorching summer's day visit this town of 600; and yes, they still offer free ice water. In the end, God did put their abilities to use and rewarded some good people when they endured until inspiration hit.

As Carla and I toured through an unending maze of rooms at Wall Drug, with every glitzy trinket of every description imaginable, we found the gem of a real chapel built into the heart of this sprawling business enterprise. Entering in, Carla and I immediately felt lifted up in this quiet respite. It is wonderful to see the goodness of everyday people who place a priority on spiritual values—even when they have become successful beyond imagination.

Another stop on our pilgrimage took us to Mt. Rushmore. This iconic sculpture made a surprising impression on both Carla and me. We both had grown up seeing pictures of these four American presidents impressively carved out of a granite cliff. The many difficulties overcome in creating this work of art are worth many stories in themselves. But here I will content myself with the effect we experienced on the day we were there.

The sculpted faces, 90 percent created with dynamite, are truly remarkable; particularly fine is George Washington's. However, it is the eyes, whose effect comes from various depths of boring into the granite that bring these faces alive. Pictures really don't convey the magnetic draw as when you are there in person.

Washington and Lincoln have always stood out first to me for their strength of character, Jefferson for his genius, and Teddy Roosevelt for his boldness and being a driving force behind the creation of National Parks.

America has played a pivotal role in the formation of Democracies around the world, but more than that, the creation of republics that have balance of power constitutions and the rule of law that both supersede and protect every individual. However imperfect these Democracies may be, they are lightyears ahead of every other form of government in recent recorded history.

The creation and preservation of this greatest of experiments—democracy—is worthy of note in the unfolding pageantry of history's march from the dark ages into more and more enlightened times. Those better times may seem far off on any particular day, but its march is sure and will one day fulfill this long-awaited prophecy.

May your own travels in life toward enlightenment be rapid and every obstacle be overcome in the face of your enduring persistence and God's grace.

Sweet chapel amidst the glitz.

September 22

REFLECTIONS ON THIS EQUINOX DAY

Greeted by a large bald eagle, Yellowstone National Park.[8]

On this Autumnal Equinox, I am put into a reflective mood. It was a year ago that we set out on a pilgrimage around North America to discover Nature's Cathedrals as well as historical sites and any and all places, persons, and situations that God arranged for us. I definitely felt that change was in the air, that the way I served God was going to be different. I did not know all the ways in which this would occur, only that it would not be the same. Flash-forward one year and it has been quite a time!

One of the great mysteries and wonders in my life in God has been the different states in which He has expressed Himself in this form since the first eruption of the kundalini force forty years ago. The question can come: is it physical, astral, or causal

---

8   On our first trail taken in Yellowstone, we were greeted by this large bald eagle—the first of many wonders on our safari-drive.

activity, or all three? For instance, tremendous heat and powerful forces in this body are a daily occurrence. At times, it can be felt hot on the skin, my face is flushed, and at other times there are absolutely no physical symptoms at all.

I had felt a weakness of the body at the end of the summer before leaving for pilgrimage a year ago. Nothing new there as God moving through this form with tremendous power can withdraw all physical energy, leaving only enough to keep the body functioning on the most basic level.

Once, for several months during the bombing and invasion of Iraq, God had me in such an intense experience that I could not move from one room to another. When Carla came into the room I was in, she said it smelled of burning flesh. This experience God was giving me was connected to events happening halfway around the world, the suffering in this body was tremendous. God's mysterious ways of working through this vehicle!

However, a year ago, it became clear that the weakness I had at the time was physical rather than spiritual. When there was no abatement of the weakness, I consulted allopathic doctors; this was the first time in many years that I was to encounter these creatures. It took time and hit-and-miss diagnoses, but finally, the cause was found: tumors growing on the small intestines that were causing internal bleeding; the weakness was from anemia. The doctor said the anemia was such that he was surprised that I could walk into the hospital. Thus, the pilgrimage took an unexpected turn.

Two major operations later and I am currently tumor-free and feel in the pink of health. Doctors fully expect the recurrence of tumors, but I know that God alone is in complete charge. I do not feel any fear about this; I am fully surrendered to His will. One of the changes that occurs in surrendering one's life to God is that fear abates, and trust ensues. What does God want for this form? He knows my own preference is to serve Him in a healthy body;

however, I also know that He works in various ways in order to achieve His purpose. I do all that I can to achieve perfect health, and indeed, in all other ways I have been in perfect health which has greatly aided my recovery.

This morning, His power took me up completely into His blissful, all-powerful Being; this, after a couple of long travel days. And now we are poised at the West Entrance of Yellowstone National Park, where we plan to explore and find His natural wonders on parade. Yellowstone, a vast caldera where superheated magma boils underground water, making for roiling, colorful paint pots and shooting geysers, is a unique place in the world. Also, Mother Nature finds expression here in bears, the ungainly-looking moose, buffalo (now the official National Mammal), and other wonders to which we plan to have darshan.

September has always been a time of change for me, and this year is no different. This continuation of the pilgrimage, earlier going to Glacier, and now the Black Hills and Yellowstone, is just one item of change. Where else will God take me? Not knowing is part of the great adventure. There was a time when God was giving me spontaneous miraculous powers, to know things in advance and manifest what came to mind, but conscious of Krishna's warning that a yogi has nothing to do with such powers, I told Him to take these things away, I only wanted Him. Truth be told, I love having things unfold and not knowing in advance (true there are times He tells me what will happen beforehand, but it is not the usual), for I trust Him with all my heart, and I have no need but what He chooses to give me at any particular moment.

An interesting sidelight, He has prompted me to purchase some beautiful things: a home that is magnificent, a motorhome that we love, and He has given us so many other things besides. It is not without irony or humor that having given everything up, from the time of entering into Cloud Mountain for a year of silence and solitude, that He has given me so much. Donations support the spiritual work, but after some legacies came to us, and after tithing the first ten percent to God, He has directed us to receive these wondrous things.

But here is the thing that God recently told me, that the home we have and all the other things He has arranged for us have been my form of Lahiri Mahasaya's castle. I have felt a deep satisfaction in experiencing the quality/vibration of these things. I truly feel that if He took them away today, I would not skip a beat. I would only be interested in all the ways He would manifest what is needed daily—as He does today and every day.

The way He takes care of us is truly so loving. Yesterday, we arrived at the West Entrance; beforehand, we could find no place in the park to make a reservation for a campsite; all were full! When we arrived, we found a campsite and started to back in when a park ranger informed us that a party had reserved the site but neglected to put up their sign. Then she asked if we wanted a site with an electrical hookup. I said that would be preferable and she rushed over in her golf cart to secure the only such site in the park! Ram looking after us so lovingly.

I know that many have found hope in the beauty—seeing what has been created in my life. Also, it is affirming that there is a balance in the spiritual life, that realization does not demand taking up residence in a cave, but can be incorporated into modern living. When God prompted me to marry Carla, I needed to test that new direction in life until I was thoroughly satisfied, down to the cellular level, that this was His will. My last big question mark was connected with Master, who held out the high value in living a monk's life. I inwardly petitioned him to confirm this inner prompting to marry, willing to give up the idea if it did not conform with his direction. In a very profound experience, he told me, unambiguously, that it was his will that I marry. That his mission required him to live a monk's life, but he wanted all to know that the spirit of Lahiri Mahasaya's life is upheld—so that all should know that being married and living a householder's life is not a bar to the highest realization.

So, this life God has given me is that demonstration, and to be in this world but not of the world is something that is within reach and can be achieved. That we live in this world knowing that whatever we have been given to be stewards over within this life will most certainly be left behind—we leave naked even as we came into life, only taking our self-created consciousness with us. A freed consciousness is forever free! Someone with a bound consciousness through attachment will continue his or her journey until, at long last, it reaches the same ultimate freedom.

These are my reflections on this Fall Equinox-day. Perhaps for you as well it is a time of new beginnings. I deeply pray that as we begin anew, as in truth we do each and every moment of every day, we establish ourselves in an unshakable freedom, a freedom that is with us no matter our circumstance in life—true, spiritual freedom, now and always.

September 25

Be Ye Perfect

Yellowstone bison with steaming pools and geysers behind.

We have been exploring a world of wonder here at Yellowstone. From placid bison grazing in valleys to elk-bucks trumpeting their call to square off in battle, a silver wolf making his way through the woods, to a large grey owl pouncing on his prey just feet away, and a trumpeter swan gliding on river's wake. We have been viewing from a seven-thousand-foot altitude an amazing blanket of stars and the river of the Milky Way seemingly without end—and that does not count geysers and hot springs that make up three-quarters of the world's supply, all within a few hours' drive.

Nature reminds us that creation operates beautifully through lawful action, but it is also brutally destructive. There was a fire here in 1988 that destroyed over a million acres of forest. On the one hand, the destruction was enormous, but the after-effect has also been tremendously creative. Lodgepole pines burst open their seeds—that only happens in the heat of a fire. The fire burned in a patchwork pattern that made reseeding happen at accelerated rates. The earth was fed with the ashes of the fire's destruction and became fertility itself. The benefits of the fire have been remarkable; also remarkable is the estimate that fewer than 300 animals perished in the enormous and out-of-control blaze.

From a human standpoint, the workings of nature can make one feel small. From a Divine perspective, it makes God extremely great. Man is definitely part of all that is; however, all that is is a marvel and more than the mind can contain. To be in awe—to be in continual awe and wonder is to be close to God.

Colorful hot springs at West Thumb.

There are many encounters with the sacred that carry with them the assurance, "Be not afraid."

Words are so difficult to encapsulate any spiritual experience within, but when in the Divine Presence, there is oftentimes, the feeling that one will be overwhelmed, that it is all too much. That is the case of the human ego trying to wrap its arms around God rather than simply surrendering to Him, to be not afraid.

We want to understand God, to know God, and really, we want to control God—that is what the human ego does in order to make itself not feel overly small or insignificant. God-experience teaches us that the human intellect is puny but the spirit within is great, so great that it can reach out to the Infinite. This reaching out can only be done through total and complete surrender, an absolute trust that lowers all defenses and barriers.

While the mind may wish to stand without reserve before the throne of the Infinite, in reality, it is actually very difficult because of years, lifetimes, of creating those very defenses. We would like to think we are in control. Obviously, there are forces far greater than we can possibly calculate. We think we can determine what is good and what is bad—out-of-control fires that burn down forests are thought to be bad. Yet the good that has come about from the enormous fire here is undeniable. On a galactical scale, suns burn up or go supernova; they also shoot out unbelievable flares across vast space, and all of these things cause great damage, yet in the total calculation of what makes for growth, these events may very well contain the seeds of new life elsewhere—can we ever really know the total good and the bad of it?

Surrounded by natural and spiritual forces that make one shrink into insignificance, we are quite often reminded that humankind is small. If the human intellect is too puny to know these things, then what are we to do? The answer: we are to be good stewards of what we do know. Still greater, in our humility, we surrender to the supreme Consciousness, the Creator of all that is, and through that surrender, do as He wills for us, oftentimes not knowing all the ways in which our thoughts, words, and actions will affect this world, but knowing deep within that it is fulfilling virtue. We only know that when we act according to the highest light in any particular situation, He may find us fit instruments to do ultimate good. We know this because we feel Him working through us, thinking through us, acting through us in perfect purity and without a trace of self.

In this hand-in-glove relationship, we are at peace, we experience bliss, we know beyond all possibility of doubt that He is the real and the true power working through every cell of our being. That is all we need know, and that fact fills us up and makes us complete.

As I write these words, I feel His power and bliss flowing through me, and my own intellect has no idea from one moment to the next as to where He is going and what He is doing next—and it is all perfect. All the wonders in this magnificent world cannot match even a moment of perfection that we can have in Spirit. But even as we discover our union in Him, Spirit reveals its perfection, and in that experience, the world is also known to be perfect.

The Lord commanded us to be perfect, and it is only when we merge into the fabric of God's Being that we can be perfect—*Perfect, even as your Father in heaven is perfect*. Nature is here to remind us of our insignificance; God is here to remind us of our greater nature, so that we can know our oneness with Him.

Great grey owl—the world's largest owl.

September 29

SACRED YELLOWSTONE

Pool at Grand Prismatic Spring.

The earth is more alive where geysers and hot boiling water are present. Because of the geyser basins and thermal areas, Yellowstone is considered to have a lot of medicine and to be a powerful spiritual place.

—EASTERN SHOSHONE CULTURAL CENTER

We have found this Shoshone saying to be true. We have visited many of Yellowstone's most famous and not-so-well-known places, and even though there have been countless visitors standing with us, it seemed there was a quietness that belied the number of people. As we waited for the Old Faithful Geyser to erupt, hundreds, perhaps thousands, lined the semi-circle walkway in hushed expectation (we could only imagine how many more people would have been here only a month ago at the height of the season).

And again, we were at the Grand Prismatic Spring as tour buses arrived with international guests in abundance from Salt Lake City, and even though there were many "shoot and shoe" tourists (barely stop to take a quick picture or selfie and then off they go!), both Carla and I felt a quiet sacredness about the place. There is a way of inwardly listening to the vibrational consciousness of a place by being quiet and receptive. Too much concern with schedules, other people around you, and other distractions, and you will miss what a place has to say to you.

We stand in awe of the dramatic colors that are vividly displayed in this most unusual setting. From minerals that erupt from the earth to the micro-organisms (*extremophiles*) that love hot pools, the colors are dazzling. These geysers and pools are what make Yellowstone a unique geology in the world.

However, it is also a wonderful place to see wildlife up close. Bison are a delightful surprise. We did not expect to have much connection with these very large mammals who spend eleven hours a day eating. They really are magnificent; as they make their way down lush river valleys, they are not only imposing, but they also have a real presence. We grew greatly fond of them, these animals that are now designated as the National Mammal of America. God fulfilled our wish to see a moose as she strolled down the river munching on the greens presenting themselves to her. And on our way back from the magnificent Grand Tetons, a large bull moose ran out of the trees next to the road in dusk's faint light. His quick reflexes and mine prevented a very problematic collision. Then he calmly continued on his way across the road—we loved seeing him from close quarters. The elk are also much admired. A female (a wapiti) made her way through some woods to come near me. Carla said she was coming to get my darshan—I thought I was there to get hers. Then the enormous bull of the herd followed her through the thicket and I made a wise retreat, as he was apparently jealous of his prerogatives!

Moose munching her way down the riverbank.

Each day has been a Ram-adventure and He has guided us perfectly. Time and again, we arrived just as something wonderful was occurring. He made sure we had a place to stay when there seemed to be none. It is not advisable to go without reservations to this first and foremost national park, but our invisible booking agent saw to everything perfectly.

Now onto our return through the Rocky Mountains. I am working on the pictures I took and will plan to put them up on the internet. The weather has been perfect fall days, even very warm the last couple of days. The painted colors of autumn are splendid, with golds of the aspen and reds of the maple making for a ridiculously vibrant palate of color. The colors are so over the top, they seem to give a glimpse into the vivacious astral worlds. This journey has certainly fulfilled the purpose of seeking out Nature's Cathedrals, and taking what the oncologist said was the best medicine for me: being in nature's wonders.

Rams in human form at the Grand Prismatic Springs; some are of the "shoot and shoe/shoo" tourist variety.

September 30

OLD MISSION—POWERFUL MEDICINE

Cataldo Mission, Idaho.

During our pilgrimage to Nature's Cathedrals, I received this email from R.B.: "Old Mission State Park in Cataldo, Idaho: Dearest David, this hallowed old Jesuit Church, built in 1850, is a priceless discovery, serving Native American tribes originally called "shee-chjo-umish," who welcomed the "Blackrobes" (their name for the Jesuit priests) into their lives. The vibration in this church is so EXTREMELY powerful! The most spiritually-charged church I have ever entered in my whole life . . . It is the humble sanctity of its vibration that still speaks to me, even today."

Needless to say, with a description like this, we felt drawn to visit this church on our way back from Yellowstone. This church, that is now a state park, keeps regular hours, and the time, as we drove over the Rocky Mountains, seemed to be dwindling. However, we crossed over into the Pacific Time Zone and a reprieve came as we gained an hour. We arrived with little under an hour to take in the site, so we skipped the museum and went straight to the wooden church built on a hilltop.

As I ascended the thick wooden stairs, I suddenly felt a spiritual magnetism envelop me. Walking through the doors, the feeling only increased. The inside was the product of simplicity, only a single row of a type of pew not usually seen. The fourteen stations of the cross in picture frames surrounded the room, the altar being rustically beautiful with sacred paintings on each end. This venerable wooden structure, which has lasted over 160 years, smelled like my grandmother's basement, but the spiritual mood was intoxicating.

Altar of the Most Sacred Heart of
Jesus (*Sacratissimi Cordis Iesu* in Latin).

I took some pictures and then joined Carla on the first, and only, seat facing the sacred heart Christ. Spontaneously, my soul silently cried, "Oh my Lord, Oh my Lord," again and again. I was nothing, He was everything. "Oh, my Lord." After some time, an inner question came from the all-pervasive Christ Consciousness, "What do you pray for?" The thought flashed for my health, but I discarded that instantly, "Oh my Lord, I pray for this world. You are all-powerful, You are everywhere present, awaken Yourself in all humanity. You are the Great Awakener, You are the eternal Light, You are the great Awakener, awaken Yourself in all humanity." And so, on went my prayer out of the depths of my soul.

So many subtly powerful experiences came in this powerfully charged house of God as my sense of being merged into His Presence, mingling with Him, yet some deep part of me continued to pray to Him—I being nothing, He being everything. Mystic Union being the only apt description. He bids me write this to you, so too must He reveal to you the depth and breadth of this moment in which time was suspended. Gradually, awareness began to creep back—somewhere, I had a body; it was in this building. Just then, the custodian came in through the back and started to close up.

We pronamed to the sacred heart and took our leave. As I dropped a donation into the box at the back of the church, the man asked, "Did you enjoy it?" It felt like it was God Himself who was asking the question; I could only nod my assent. He said, "Good." As with R.B., the grace of the Old Mission stays with me still, and as I write this, I am wrapped in the powerful experience I had there.

Joseph holding young Jesus' hand.

Priest's alcove off to the side of the altar.

Note: The Coeur d'Alene tribe asked for priests to come to them after hearing they were powerful medicine men in black robes. The church was constructed by the natives, and the structure was made with the wattle and daub method: no nails were used at all on this long-lasting wood structure. Cut-down tin cans fabricated the candle holders; painted newspaper that had been sent to the priest made for wallpaper; the blue-colored wood was stained using pressed huckleberries, and the statues were carved using only a knife. Antonio Ravalli, an Italian Jesuit, designed the mission building. Obviously, there have been tremendous souls surcharging this church. A description of a gathering of old natives emphasized their great devotion. Here is an example of the union of two cultures that served to spiritually surcharge this mission building that today carries with it the Christ's great Presence.

October 2

First Yellowstone Safari

Noble Bison: Two-thousand-pound survivor from the last Ice Age.

After securing a campsite at Baker's Hole, just outside the West Entrance to Yellowstone, it is a day of chores and getting settled in. We then take in the excellent museum and park visitor center in West Yellowstone. It is now evening, but we are anxious to at least drive a little into the park in our rented jeep. So off we go, gradually realizing that this is an excellent time of day to see the animals as the coolness of evening brings them out; we are driving next to the Madison River where the larger animals like to come and drink and eat the sweet grass.

The first turnoff shows some promise of a view of the river and has a boardwalk built for that purpose. Our attention is drawn to an enormous bald eagle on a snag across the flowing river. We walk down to, and along, the river for further sights. Then we return for a closer view of the eagle. I walk a little closer to the

river for a picture; just then, he turns his head in my direction—beautiful shot. "Thank you, Mr. Eagle, for your darshan."

Large eagle gives me his darshan.

Onward we drive, with most of the traffic going out of the park
in the opposite direction—good for us. A car that has stopped
on the road in front of us alerts us to a bull bison just to the side.
These majestic creatures were once numbered in the millions,
with one herd counting in at a million buffaloes that stretched
sixty miles in length! They had been hunted to near extinction for
a variety of reasons: one was the value of their pelts and leather,
and the second came towards the end when it was seen as a way
to resolve "the Indian problem," forcing native tribes onto reservations by robbing them of the food, shelter, and tools that the
buffaloes provided. The number in the park was reduced to twen-
ty-five buffaloes, a few hundred in total were left when the army
stepped in to preserve the few survivors.

These beasts are enormous, weighing in at a ton for males,
half a ton for females. Strong and limber, jumping a six-foot high
obstacle from a standing position and running 35 miles per hour,
they are a fearsome product of nature. Buffaloes have the distinc-
tion of having survived the last ice age and have outlasted many of

the other animals of that time period. Today, the herds number in the tens of thousands, and a problem now takes place when they wander off the Park grounds and are the unwelcomed guests of ranchers and homeowners—imagine one or more of these two-thousand-pounders munching on your lawn or wandering in the playground of the local elementary school! Having the pleasure of the darshan of this noble wonder, we drive on.

A few cars from our direction stop and a corresponding traffic jam of a mile or more coming from the other way indicates a herd of elk just off the side of the road on the strip of land that spans a few hundred feet down to the river. A large bull elk and his harem are moving down the grassy slopes and through the pine trees on a leisurely graze. We stop to get out and see these wild ones closer up (but careful to be not too close). As we stand at a distance, a female wapiti (a term for elk from the Shawnee, meaning white rump) comes near to me. Carla, who quickly retreats, says the cow is coming for my darshan. The head bull is not pleased with this proximity and also moves towards me through the trees to warn away any uninvited visitors—that being me! I gracefully make my way back. The bull herds the cow back into his comfort zone. Just how big this bull is and how powerfully he moves is even more evident when he has me in his sights!

We motor on and come to a wide-open field at the confluence of the Madison and the Fire Hole Rivers (called a prayag in India—a holy site), where a buffalo (formal name is bison) is off in the field. Carla has been keen to see buffalo, so we stop. There is also a herd of elk down by the river. We stalk the buffalo for a while then head down to the river toward the elk. There is a very large bull and many cows, with another younger bull also in attendance.

Bull elk has me in his sights.

The sun sets on this charming scene, and we sit on a bench watching the various actors in this scenario, including a few human varieties. With increasing regularity, the large bull elk bugles his call, an unusual and very loud sound. Off in the distance, we hear another bull elk also bugling—someone walking by suggests there may be another herd nearby.

As this scene continues to unfold, a single bull elk appears off to our left and it becomes obvious that he is the origin of the other bugle calls. Now, this is getting quite interesting—both bulls are making alternating calls; it seems a challenger for one, or all, of the females has found his way to the herd. By the size of his antlers, he is large, but not quite as large as the current head of the herd, who surely weighs in at over a thousand pounds. Autumn is mating season when the males are in rut (rut is derived from Latin meaning roar, or the bugling sound they make).

Large bull elk bugling in defense of his harem.

There are two females who are outliers from the herd, and they seem to be the object of this challenger. We move down to the riverside and watch in breathless anticipation as the two bulls grow closer, each making tremendous noise. The larger bull is slowly moving toward the challenger. We have little knowledge of their mating and challenging habits, so all of this is an extraordinary play unfolding before us. Clashing horns is not a usual part of the challenge, but a display of antlers, bugling, and posturing is effective in eventually making the challenger break off his pursuit of the one cow further up in the woods. However, he now makes his way across the river toward us in pursuit of the other cow.

Carla makes a wise retreat, and I have a few small trees next to me to use as defense if that should be necessary. The larger bull then comes across the creek as well and successfully defends his other cow, although she seems interested in the newcomer.

Finally, prompted by his bull calls, grunts (typical male), and movements toward her, the female seems to come out of her entrancement with the newcomer and runs back across the river downstream where the rest of the herd is grazing down the valley. All of this has been taking place for the past thirty or forty minutes and has kept us spellbound.

By now, it is getting very dark, and a forest ranger has arrived at the nearby Madison Creek Campground to give a talk and slideshow on the Bison. We decide to stay for that. After a fascinating presentation, we make the forty-minute drive in the dark back to our campsite. Although we had a late start to our safari for our first day in the park, Ram has seen to it that it was a thriller. It really is remarkable how much can be packed into a relatively short amount of time when God is the tour guide!

October 19

A Meditation on Master

Loon Lake seen through forest trees.**

A spiritual retreat is a concentrated time of companionable connections and deepened divine awareness—I only wish that all could attend. Each retreat is a mystery as to what the topic will be. As the date approached, my prayer was that our time together would fulfill the highest good of all—whatever topic God chose.

The approach of the 70th anniversary of the release of the *Autobiography of a Yogi* in December of this year triggered the topic—to spend our time meditating on the life and ongoing influence of our great master, Paramhansa Yogananda. When a soul such as Sri Yoganandaji realizes God, his life yields an unending source of inspiration and offers unlimited facets of a divine personality.

I asked our three ministers to read passages from the *Autobiography of a Yogi* that were particularly meaningful to them. Larry focused on the fascinating chapter, *Kashi, Reborn and Rediscovered.* It is an intense experience for Master as he promises to do a thing that he is not sure how to do—to find Kashi in his new incarnation and put him solidly on the spiritual path. Through his knowledge of how the heart acts as a receiving station and the ajna a transmitter, Master develops a method for finding Kashi that he fearlessly and relentlessly employs in order to fulfill his sacred promise.

That promise is made when Kashi asks about his future. Master spontaneously says *You shall soon be dead.* Instead of Kashi asking that his life be spared, he implores Master to find him when he reincarnates and ensure his continued spiritual journey. Kashi is unremitting in pursuing Master to fulfill this difficult occult request. Master finally relents when he sees Kashi stretched to the breaking point. It is both touching and fascinating as Master describes in humble detail how he fulfills his sacred promise to his beloved disciple.

Jill read from the chapter, *The Resurrection of Sri Yukteswar,* in which Master's guru describes the afterlife, and in particular, the astral worlds. In his new afterlife role, Sri Yukteswarji serves as spiritual preceptor in an astral heaven where he is a guru for those souls who leave their bodies on earth in a high state of realization, but are not yet fully realized. The great master intimately knows the comings and goings *in all the three worlds.* Jill spoke about her younger days when she was keenly aware of death, a constant feature of life, but no one wanted to talk about it. Death, the elephant in the room that went unnoticed, was finally addressed when she read the Autobiography. It spoke deeply to her long-held quest to know the truth about death.

Peter described that when he was given the Autobiography as a young teen, it struck him as the ultimate adventure story. Master ran away from home to the Himalayas in search of saints as a youth. Peter could identify with this impulse and in reading the Autobiography, he felt he was on an exciting spiritual journey with Mukunda. Peter related how his awakened spiritual life helped him in an outdoor adventure of his own in the Alaskan wilderness. He and a friend hiked and then paddled a raft to a campsite at the end of a remote lake. The plan was for a seaplane to pick them up in three days. They were well prepared; however, when they unpacked, there were no matches! Their freeze-dried food was inedible without the required hot water, so they faced the daunting prospect of no food and no warming fire in the days to come.

The two young campers displayed an unusual response to this crisis—both entered into a deepened state of prayer. After placing their dilemma before God, they searched around a bit and discovered matches mysteriously spread on the ground, and amazingly, quite amazingly, they were dry and flame-worthy. How could these matches inexplicably be in this remote area and in perfect condition? This demonstration of God's Grace was not dissimilar to what happened in Master's life that he describes in the chapter Peter read: *Two Penniless Boys in Brindaban*. Master's life ignited a spiritual flame in young Peter that has burned ever since.

The retreat was filled with Master, his grace definitely felt. No better topic could have surfaced for our time together, and it is positive proof that Master is a living presence that only grows with time.

Mother Hamilton's personal copy
of the *Autobiography of a Yogi*.

October 23

Blessings—Not Luck

Hindu God Ganesh: Remover of
Obstacles. Statue in Bhubaneswar, India.**

What do we mean when we say, "Good luck?" We are wishing someone well, that things go well. And what does it mean for "things to go his or her way"? We all know there are times in life when everything seems to just go easier, contrasted to other times when it feels like one difficulty after another is trying to stop us. Good luck means either the impediments disappear or that they are overcome.

But why any impediments at all? Is it bad luck that is at fault? The same person with the same body conditioning may be walking down a slight hill, talking, smiling, and laughing all along the way, or they may be climbing a steep incline where all talk ceases, the lungs act like overworked bellows, and the person feels as though he or she will not make it to the top! Is the hill climbed bad luck?

When we find individuals who are struggling to put one foot in front of the other, we want them to have strength, endurance, to have some things go their way. Each individual may focus upon his or her own abilities; however, to the thoughtful person, it becomes clear that every individual is connected to something higher, and events that swirl all around have a Source beyond random chance—there is a Creator, a God. Rather than ascribing this source to luck, we ultimately want another to be blessed by the giver of all good things. Good luck really means: *God bless you.*

If we would but know it, all things in our life are a result of the law of cause and effect, the law of karma. However, higher than the law of karma, or the stars, genetics, or any other influence from the material world is the power, intelligence, and grace that comes directly from Divine Consciousness.

Replacing *no, I can't consciousness* with *yes, I will consciousness* is a tremendous step in evolution. But a giant leap forward comes in uniting individual will with the supreme Creator's will, which makes all things possible. Light is stronger than the dark, love more powerful than fear, omniscience true and separation false; in all ways, the Presence of God is superior to anything this world offers.

It is the human mind that is the battleground for these two ways of perceiving the source for overcoming—the human and the Divine. Years and lifetimes of survival mode make us think we must rely only upon our own wits and capabilities. And, although it becomes clear there is a Divine Consciousness that is the true source of our being, past programming remains strong in feeling, *it is just me.*

My own journey in knowing this *something higher* began when I was a late teen. My own decision-making and circumstances led me to a crisis of great emotional pain. In the middle of the night, I sat in the front yard looking at the starry sky, feeling my heart splitting in two in the most painful way possible. It was so painful that I prayed, "God, I don't know if you exist, but if you do, if I have never needed you before, I need you now. Please, help me with this pain!" Immediately, I felt as if a thousand-pound weight was lifted from my shoulders and the pain in my heart was alleviated.

My rational mind argued that there was no divine intervention, but a deeper part of me could not deny it, I knew that it was. This was a momentary opening of a door to a much greater way of being. The way was slow and bumbling, but a seed was planted in the rocky ground of doubt and denial. It found enough good soil that it eventually bore a tree of realization. The most tremendous change began when I was blessed on that warm summer's night.

Instead of wishing you good luck, I see, in the depth of my communion with the all-beneficent Lord of creation, that you are blessed—most particularly that your journey to the highest realization is greatly quickened. In that spirit, God's greatest blessings to you.

October 28

ARJUNA CHOOSES KRISHNA

Krishna Tells the Gita to Arjuna**

A nger can be one of our greatest tests on the way up in our search for God-consciousness. Either a deep rage or a brooding discontent interferes with our connection to the Divine. When we analyze it, we come to know that anger is caused by attachment to how things *are supposed to be*. If you think traffic is supposed to be moving fast and there is a sudden stoppage, a flare of rage may erupt. It is the thought that traffic should be flowing at high speed, and then it is not, that causes the disturbance.

In our desire to continuously experience the qualities of the Divine, we must cut the binding cord of attachment. In this work of letting go, we differentiate between attachment and having an ideal. We can have the ideal that there should be no violence in this world, that everyone should work their problems out non-violently. Yet, we find ourselves in a world where violence is all too prevalent. I have known those who are very disturbed by the violence in this world, and in their disturbance, they are livid. Their thoughts and emotions emit violence in their rage. How can they bring peace to this world when they have none of it themselves?

In the Mahabharata, the epic poem from India, there is a collision of forces that ends up in a massive war involving millions. Krishna belongs to one of the royal families drawn into the conflict. He first attempts to mediate a solution, but when King Duryodhana is insistent on maintaining an unrighteous position, Krishna makes the decision to bequeath his army to one side, and that he, unarmed, will stand with the other. Arjuna (self-control) is first to choose, he takes Krishna, not his army. King Duryodhana (material desire) thanks his lucky stars that his enemy Arjuna has picked Krishna, leaving Krishna's army for himself.

Duryodhana is recklessly angry, trying to prove himself and find security through his position in the world. Arjuna is calmly determined and looks to Krishna as his guide. Arjuna does not yet realize that Krishna is a divine incarnation; however, he does know that Krishna is wise and very special; he definitely wants him by his side. Though the battles are hard-fought, and many times go against Arjuna, eventually, he and his side win the war.

The key is that he has asked Krishna to be the driver of his chariot. Although in a worldly sense a charioteer is beneath the dignity of royalty, Krishna accepts the position. Spiritually, this puts him in command of Arjuna on the battlefield. It is Krishna who teaches and directs Arjuna. Arjuna fights without anger; neither does he give into despondency. He fights because it is God's direction to do so, to fulfill righteousness.

We find in Arjuna exactly the right attitude in life. This world is a battlefield of competing interests, and to run away leaves the field to those who are driven by lower desires. If good people do not become policemen, then those posts are left to scoundrels and the world suffers. This is true of all positions, from the janitor to CEOs of large companies, political leaders, and spiritual ministers. Dharma, right action, betters the world, adharma, wrong motives, brings suffering.

The essential factor is that you must serve with a focus upon doing what is right, putting God's direction in the driver's seat. When you are driven by angry vitriol or seething revenge, no good can come of it. When you stand aside out of fear or tepidness, the world suffers. To find the right balance of calm, decisive action based upon the highest light you know will produce the highest and best results for yourself and the world at large. Determine to demonstrate your Arjuna within—put God first and enter into the world to do what is right, with all your might.

November 2

GATHERING GOD

Shiva, king of meditating yogis, at *Kailash Nath Temple, Murugeshpayla, Bangalore.***

People naturally gather information of various kinds: an avid baseball fan analyzes the statistics of various players, an intellectual gleans facts and information from his favorite subjects, a philosopher studies and compares the stages of history, and so on. Our spiritual journey is composed of a different kind of "gathering."

In the beginning, an aspirant may study various religions, teachers, and philosophies. However, as one deepens in merging the

little self into the vast Self, the mind takes on a different purpose from that of gathering information. Now the mind is used
to focus attention upon transcending the mind through a mantra or some other meditational focus. Experience teaches that
only when the mind is still is God revealed—this making all the
difference.

No longer is gathering facts and information central to the
aspirant's life. With full awareness, the mind becomes still; the
little bubble of the self dissolves and merges into the vast ocean
of Consciousness. Now pure Consciousness is known, the one
without a second. This pure awareness resides in its Self: no
thought, no information gathering, no reference to another; it is
purna: whole and complete.

When I started this journey of journeys, I had many questions
about so many things. Some of these questions could not be
answered by books or intellectual study; they could only come
from a source beyond speculation. As I continued in this quest, I
found so many of those questions were either answered, or they
simply dropped off—the growing stillness rendered questions
obsolete.

This morning I entered the inner Temple of Silence, the thought
of the bubble dissolving into the sea made it so. Whatever defines
this part of the mind that operates in the world simply disinte-
grates; awareness becomes a vast ocean of consciousness. It is
not an empty ocean; it is full of all life, everything that is good and
pure; it has no need for activity, so it rests in the bliss and peace
of itself.

To the worldly mind, this may seem like a nice dream, or it
may be inconceivable how one could be enraptured when there
is no constant stimulation. My mom said, when I told my parents
I was going into silence and seclusion for the next year, that she
imagined if my father tried that he would run out of the cabin in a

few days, desperate to know the score of the football game! Most would have their version of a driving need to know the score—news of a child or grandchild, of the world, work, friends, or family.

There is the story told in India of the yogi who simply showed up at a temple and spent his days meditating. The temple fed the yogi daily, and for the rest of his time, he meditated or rested. The wealthy man who financed the temple noticed this yogi and that he did not do any chores around the temple, simply ate his meals and seemed to do nothing else. Finally, he had had enough of this and angrily approached the yogi. "You do not do anything here. You should leave!" he shouted. The yogi was calm in the face of this verbal assault and answered, "I will gladly leave, but I would like you to meditate with me for a little while first." The businessman said he did not have time for such foolishness, but the yogi was somehow calmly insistent and prevailed. The businessman spent some uncomfortable minutes trying to sit still, but could not. Suddenly, it dawned on him what "work" this yogi was doing by meditating long hours throughout the day—he gained a newfound respect for him. "Mahatma," the businessman said, "you may remain here at this temple as long as you like, blessing it's precincts with your dedicated meditation."

In your practice, you recognize that what you are doing is fundamentally different from what a worldly man or woman does. From the depths of your meditation, you may very well be inspired to do some great work; however, you must know God first for any endeavor to be truly successful. To know God, you transcend the desires, thoughts, and all preoccupations of the self. First, merge your little self in the great Self of God, then let all action flow from that high state. You will certainly be a blessing to this whole world as no other can be.

November 6

Come—Rise Up

Mother Hamilton, portrait from 1960s.**

The mind directs our life-energy, emotions, and moods; change the mind and all else will follow. My football coach of old taught us a move called a head-shuck. When the opposing player came right at you, the forearm was to be applied to the side of his head with some force—moving his head to one side or the other. The coach confidently told us that wherever the head went—the rest of the body would follow! I never saw that principle proved wrong.

So, with your mind, wherever it goes, the rest of you will follow. Change your thoughts, change your life. The complication comes in that people's minds are "a house divided." That is, the mind becomes fractured and can actually oppose itself. When President Harry Truman consulted economists about what policies he should institute, he heard, "Well, on the one hand, we can do this, but on the other hand, we could do that. Finally, the exasperated president exclaimed, "What I would give for a one-handed economist!" There are two sides to every thought; that is its nature.

The only way to the deeper truth of any subject is through refined intuition. Certainly, the reasoning mind plays an important role in gathering information and performing analysis, but that part of the brain can never ascertain absolute higher meaning. For that, truth is known in deeper states of meditation, which opens a doorway to a greater reality.

Intuition of this sort is not simply a mental flash or idea. It is an experience that uplifts and transforms you. The fact that there are those who claim to have divine inspiration and are clearly deluded only demonstrates that we must be very good spiritual scientists, not sloppy or inauthentic. The number of times it has been predicted that the world would be destroyed or civilization would collapse on a particular day and time, then nothing occurred at the appointed moment, has baffled more than one observer as to how such charlatans get a hearing at all. The fact is, fear sells, as the news reporters demonstrate daily.

Many times, revelations from God are not at all dramatic in nature, but elucidate a simple truth that high drama cannot compete with. Reflect on the time when Jesus talked about the lilies of the field, remarking that Solomon, in all of his glory, was not arrayed as one of these (Luke 12:27). What was Jesus' experience when he looked at a small lily that made him talk like this? What a tremendous vision he must have had that speaks to us still, thousands of years later.

Many times, I have a revelation that defies speech. I could say the words, but you would not comprehend the enlightenment that is behind them. Only a direct revelation would accomplish the shared realization. While we benefit from reading the words of the spiritually great, seeing the words alone cannot lift us into the high state from which those words were uttered.

I remember listening to Mother talk and thinking to myself, "I want to be in the same state of consciousness in hearing those words as Mother is when she is speaking them." In truth, this is why Mother was saying those words in the first place, to lift me into the bliss, wisdom, and light she was enjoying.

Come, rise up into the consciousness of Krishna, Christ, Yogananda, Mother; know the same state of awareness they know; be infused with the same power to bring light and healing to one and to all; immerse yourself into the bliss they too enjoyed. It is the reason they taught at all, so that you might be as they are in God. Come, receive your innate divinity and be one with your heavenly Father and Divine Mother.

November 9

THE LOVE OF GOD

Mother Hamilton gave the love of
God to all. Photo from Seattle, c. 1976.

Truly speaking, it is not that we have to love God; we have
to know that God who is Love is enthroned in our hearts.
By surrendering ourselves to this Divine Love in us, we
become embodiments of that Love. By constant remembrance and meditation, we realize His presence in us, and
our life becomes filled with His light and love. His love
then radiates through us, and we see with love, talk with
love, give with love, receive with love and act with love.

—SWAMI RAMDAS

This great saying by Papa is really tremendous. So, what does it mean when we hear elsewhere that we must love God in order to know Him? There are two stages for the *love of God:* one is from the aspiring human viewpoint, and the other is totally Divine. Human *love of God* means you aspire, pray, and love God more than the world. That is, you have an overwhelming need and drive for God-consciousness, truth, bliss, expansive awareness, and Universal Vision that supersedes your greedy, lustful, self-centered way of life. This striving for higher consciousness uses the power of attraction that is generated by powerful love to purify your mind and lift you into the supreme consciousness of God.

Achieving union with God makes the second stage of the *love of God* a living reality. You are now merged in universal Divine Love. Love naturally pours through your heart; love guides and enlightens you; it effortlessly flows through every part of your being in thought, word, and action. Divine Love is now part and parcel of your being.

This past week was spent in Ashland with a beautiful group of flowering devotees and aspirants, all coming together in Satsang—a Sanskrit term that means: Sat-truth, and sang-gathering, gathering together to immerse ourselves in the highest truth. In the midst of these sincere seekers, the love of God radiated and flowed through my heart and soul without limit.

Mother said that she gave to all the love of God. Today I understand that differently than I did when I first heard Mother say it. Although I could feel love, such as I had never experienced before, flowing from Mother, I had no idea of the source of that love or what she must be experiencing when she said it. Now I can say, from my own experience, I give the love of God to all, and it is the most magnificent experience—a way of seeing God in action.

My heart is wide open as love flows like a vast river. There is no beginning or end, only radiant love shines and moves through to one and all. It has no demand, nor does it need reciprocity; however, it glows brightly when there is receptivity in another. It is strong in the physical presence of someone or a group, but it is equally powerful from a distance as well. When I think of another who is far away, there is a distinct awareness that love is transmitted directly to the recipient.

There are literally no barriers; even what we call death is no bar to the power of this love. It is not sentimentality, nor is it blind or deluded; rather, it is transcendent and knows the worth of another far better than what the faculties of our senses or mind can comprehend.

Whether you are practicing loving God in order to attain Him, or you are immersed in Divine Love through realization, love will be found to be the most potent force in all the three worlds. To remain in a sterile world empty of emotion is not proof against suffering; it is only through union with God that you will know that freedom. If you ask, "Where is this love you speak of?" It is here, within you, and all around you, you are verily swimming in an ocean of love, and always have been—you need only receive it.

November 13

WALKING AMONG GIANTS

Redwood Forest, Northern California.

We mark Armistice Day, the signing of peace between the Allies and Germany that ended WWI in 1918, every year on 11–11 (November 11th) at 11 a.m. It was a day of celebration for the Allies and a symbol of peace for what was touted to be *the war to end all wars*—how wrong that proved to be. It is still a day to remember—for those who sacrificed much as well, it is a day of peace. This is also the anniversary of the birth of Swamiji Satchidananda, to whom so much is owed.

On this anniversary day, I walk among giants. We are here in northern California in the Redwood National and State Parks—entering one of nature's great cathedrals. A remarkable aspect of Redwood trees concerns time. The oldest of these living trees can be traced back to before the time of Jesus, and the ancestors of these sequoia redwoods stood tall during the time of dinosaurs! While strolling beneath these pillars of the forest, some reaching over 300 feet high, my attention is naturally drawn skyward, as well as making me think of long stretches of time, at least by human standards.

This reflection on time put me in a train of thought about the affairs of humans. My brief visit—hours of walking in a couple of days—would barely register by redwood standards. However, even in this short time, the clear sense of soulfulness in these *Sequoia sempervirens* is abundantly apparent. These ancients exude longevity, a perspective that makes human calculation based on the minute, hour, and day seem all too insignificant. What are years compared to millennia, was it not 1918 only a moment ago?

Certainly, each person's perspective is important to them; a moment can make time stand still or a lifetime can be over in the blink of an eye. Even the millennial view, however long by our standards, is still only a blink of an eye in eternity. And this is where time becomes a plaything. It is relative to the state of consciousness we have in the moment. Whether time has come to a stop, is crawling or flying by, whether we think in expansive geological time or measure the microseconds of a sprinter, the concept of time is pliable and ultimately dependent on the individual.

Our ascent into Divine Consciousness proves that time and timelessness are completely dependent on shifts of consciousness. The soul may rise up and know that time is suspended when absorbed in transcendent awareness. The Over-Soul has ever been; it is now, and it will ever be. This is not a mere philosophical concept, but an obvious reality to the all-conscious Self. Even as God-consciousness can span the space of a far-reaching galaxy or even the universe itself, and then be found to be equally present in the miniscule atom, so can the Divine be in vast reaches of time, or in the eternal moment of now. For God-consciousness is transcendent to, and immanent in, both time and space. It is the great equalizer to omniscience; the life of a flower is on equal footing with the life of a stellar system, or even a universe.

Peace is not something that occurs at any particular time, such as when an agreement is signed; peace is an ever-existent state of being that can be made self-evident at any and all times. Just as a state of Self-realization is not something to achieve, such as making something new, rather it is something you have always been, only are unaware of it. We think that the world can one day be made perfect, but it is already perfect! A newborn is perfect, and so are a child and a young adult; through all stages, the individual is perfect just as he or she is, only that one may not be aware of it; that is all. You would not say, while watching a play, that it is imperfect without seeing it to its end; only at the conclusion can you properly ascertain its worth—and so it is with life.

The feeling of peace and the perspective of time I experience while hiking in this forest is one of life's great experiences. Just so, you may know peace now—whatever your circumstances; it is your eternal gift. As I meander in awe at the feet of these grand beings, I feel their ancient wisdom in the simple quiet. They awaken in me through the thought, "What is a moment? See what a brief speck time is. Know the eternal verities if you would be wise: patient awareness, silence, stillness with vibrant life-energy resounding; stand straight and reach for the heavens while rooted in the earth and draw strength from kindred spirits." These are whispered truths that seep deeply into my soul from their souls, as I walk among giants.

Redwoods: get their color from tannin, which protects the trees from insects, fungi, and fire. Redwoods can absorb half of their water needs from fog. The roots of the trees are relatively shallow; however, they get much of their grounded strength from interweaving their roots with other redwoods. These giants have a tiny seed, only about an inch long. Much of their new growth is a result of cloning via a bulbous formation that activates when the main tree is damaged. This formation will grow a new tree genetically identical to the original. A redwood called the General Sherman is, by volume, the largest tree in the world.

Yogacharya David standing among
one of the medium-sized brothers.

November 20

He Must Come to You

Swami Ramdas: In continuous
remembrance of Ram Nam.

The notion of a mantra or chanting as a means for achieving states of higher consciousness is well known in the East, but is only beginning to be explored in more recent years here in the West. A chant used for this purpose normally does not have many lyrics; it does not tell a story or have a romantic appeal—rather, its simplicity is its power.

Recently, a dear devotee was inspired by a statement Mother Hamilton had made, "If you call upon the name of the Lord for 24 hours unceasingly, He cannot refuse to answer. He *must* come to you." Originally, she thought to start chanting Ram Nam unceasingly the day after her long workday, but God prompted her to start immediately after, 11:00 that night. She asked for blessings for her accomplishment of this noble endeavor. I suggested anytime tiredness affected her, that she walk and chant for some time.

It is interesting that God's prompting made her chant throughout the night of a supermoon, a time when the full moon was the closest to the earth (perigee) since 1948, and would not be this close again until 2034, a unique night for spiritual practice. Spiritually, full moons are considered favorable; it was on a full moon that the Buddha achieved nirvana and it was on a full moon that the gopis met Krishna in a dance of divine ecstasy.

Her practice brought to mind times at Anandashram, especially on full moon nights, when I climbed to the top of Manjupati, the hill behind the ashram, and chanted through the night. On one such night, I was unsuccessfully trying to remember a new chant I had heard at the ashram when suddenly some distant temple in the valley below played over loudspeakers the very Ram Nam tune I had been trying to remember! (Only in India would a temple play a chant at this volume at two in the morning!) In heart-melting gratitude to the Infinite Beloved for answering this smallest of desires in such a unique way, I looked out on the night, with dots of lighted lamps here and there below, in the distance incoming waves of the Arabian Sea reflecting the moon's light, and with a shawl wrapped around me for warmth in the rare coolness, Ram Nam kept me company and lifted me into His Presence throughout the nocturnal observance. On other nights, when there was a 24-hour Ram Nam at the mandirs for some special occasions, I walked the ashram walkways to quietly chant during the night.

I felt in sympathetic connection throughout for this beloved aspirant during her 24-hour practice. After this "experiment," she felt no tiredness; rather, she was *rested in a complete way*. When drowsiness did come, she walked and chanted and did some yoga stretches without loss of Ram Nam, which was continuous. She also felt a deepened guru-disciple connection. From my own previous experiences, I know this dedicated period of practice will reverberate into the future, strengthening her ongoing remembrance of God.

Ram Nam practice takes the aspirant through a number of stages. From the beginning, chanting Ram Nam has given me a feeling of upliftment, peace, and bliss. This purification results in continuous God-experience—feeling His presence permeating mind, body, and spirit. At a certain point, the vibration of Ram Nam enters the spine, awakening an awareness of a vast inner space filled with sacredness. The illumined spine and brain then effortlessly merge with outer creation—God within, God without. This universal vision confirms that there is no place where God is not.

When every cell of your being resonates with the divine feeling, you may be sure you are in God-consciousness. You know that you are not the body, not any temporary emotional state, and you are beyond thought—you are eternal Spirit existing in a state of freedom. The power of chanting is just becoming more widely known, but what a power it unleashes to lift one and all into the bliss of His Presence—through continuous and earnest practice, *He must come to you.*

Note: Since we returned from the Redwoods, God has kept me in a powerful inner experience that keeps me indrawn in Him. It is, for this reason, I am not giving a talk this Sunday, the week of Thanksgiving. Know that I am with you in spirit.

November 23

A NATURAL STATE OF GRATITUDE

Yogacharya David, Anandashram, India, 2005**

Gratitude can transform common days into thanksgivings, turn routine jobs into joy, and many opportunities into blessings.

—WILLIAM ARTHUR WARD (1921–1994)

Experiencing Divine Grace begets a natural state of gratitude, even as a sense of gratitude brings about a feeling of closeness with our Creator. To have a day set aside for giving thanks is a wonderful idea, but with feasts, football, and family, is there even a moment set aside for honoring the spirit of the holiday? Sri Yoganandaji advocated a time for both a social Christmas and a meditative spiritual Christmas; likewise, we can take time to honor the spirit of Thanksgiving with family, and take time to deepen our inner communion with God.

Reflecting on the news-media, our minds can become fixated upon the things that are troubling about the world. However, there truly is much to be thankful for. In the year Mother Hamilton was born, 1904, the average life expectancy world-wide was 32 years, 20 percent of newborn children did not make it to see their first birthday, and the average income was $2,000 a year (in today's dollars). Flash-forward a hundred years: global life-expectancy is 70 years, first-year deaths have been reduced to 3.6 percent, and the average person now makes $10,070. Even in the last twenty years, global poverty has fallen by half (when they polled people about this one fact, only 5 percent guessed that it was cut in half; the rest thought it had marginally improved, was the same, or worse). Another improved area in the U.S. is in polluting emissions, which have dropped 70 percent since 1970, while the economy has grown 240 percent. There is much to be grateful for.

While material improvements in health and prosperity are important, they are incomplete in themselves. Without the core of deepened spirituality, these outer improvements are hollow, the sounding of a thin tin bell. Only through deepened communion with the Almighty does that sound become enriching—a beautifully toned bell, reverberating for all the ages. The gift of spiritual awakening is the ultimate gift for which we are grateful. Just getting started on this path to Self-realization is of great import; how many darkened lifetimes have we spent in ignorance and suffering with no spiritual understanding?

To be given quality tools for realization and guidance from an extraordinary lineage is reason enough for giving profound thanks. However, like the negative popular news about this world, you can focus on those things in life you do not like about yourself without acknowledging the progress you have made. Giving gratitude brings about balance in your perspective; look at all the ways you have grown, advanced, and become more empowered! Taking legitimate pride in what you have done circles you, the sincere aspirant, right back to the source of your accomplishments—your life in God.

On this day of thanksgiving, I have gratitude for having a body in good health, which is remarkable after what has occurred in the past year. Thanks to your support, loving thoughts, and sincere prayers, as well as excellent medical care, I am still very much here. Which leads to another area of gratefulness. When I first started this spiritual journey, I had no compatriots in Spirit. Over time, Mother drew me to herself, and, through her, to so many sincere aspirants—as kindred spirits upon the path, you are my treasured gifts. God has given us each other to make spiritual progress with and to give mutual support—what a tremendous gift that has been in my life. For that, and for all the unbounded grace God gives, I am deeply grateful.

I wish you deepened connection with God and Gurus as you mindfully keep your own day of thanksgiving.

November 27

Tis the Season

Santa Claus created by Lois Hickenbottom.

For those of us in the largely Christian West, we have entered the Christmas Season: ostensibly celebrating the birth of Jesus. As with many religions that spread to new lands, folk traditions often become incorporated into the newly accepted faith; so, among other things, many of us will have Christmas trees in our homes.

Yesterday, we put our tree up, complete with lights and the delight of bringing out of storage decorations—many of which have special meaning. This early morning, I sit in otherwise complete darkness with the lighted tree shining—and with it, there is a magic spell that comes to life. It is this special feeling that enhances so much of the power behind the traditions and celebrations of Christmas.

We love to see the look of wonder in our small children, and through that, to re-awaken in ourselves the experience of *magic.* Without a focus on the underlying power of these traditions, we can get caught up in the externals of buying gifts, going to parties, and all the tradition that goes with this season. The feelings of awe and magic are tender shoots that can be choked out by the pernicious weeds of excess, greed, competition, alcohol, drugs, and getting caught up in being too busy and having too many commitments to *do it all.*

Whew, take a breath! I am far from *bah-humbug,* for I love this season of lights in darkness, listening to Handel's Messiah and other favorite music associated with the season, and watching movies such as "It's A Wonderful Life," "Jesus of Nazareth," and "Scrooge" (I especially like Alistair Sim).[9] I am also aware that in trying to capture the magic of the season, we may lose focus on what is essential, allowing those noxious weeds to strangle those very tender feelings right out of existence.

That feeling of *magic and awe* we love to see in children—is not for children only! It is unfortunate that because we use fanciful stories and contrivance to evoke that feeling in children, we can quash that very needed quality with our adult view of *realism.* We can turn it all around, inside out, and be repulsed by the excesses, become the *bah-humbug* of Mr. Scrooge. Of course, the fully adult version of *magic and awe* comes with loving God—in fact, we do our children a disservice by not teaching them this "reality" from

---

9   *A Christmas Carol,* later released as *Scrooge* (1951). George Minter Productions. Directed by Brian Desmond Hurst. *A Wonderful Life* (1946). Liberty Films. Directed by Frank Capra. *Jesus of Nazareth* (1977). ITC Entertainment. RAI. Directed by Franco Zeffirelli.

the beginning. When our whole being is lit up with the eternal Light, we become a finely decorated tree with the spine as the trunk and the nerves as the branches. The Star of the East is seen at the Christ Center of the ajna, and gifts are delivered when those fine spiritual feelings are felt throughout our beings. Christ is born anytime the Presence of God is felt and there are acts of loving service.

We honor the season best when we dive deep into meditation to find the Source of that most powerful feeling of *magic and awe*. Then we will be mindful to not allow noxious weeds to drown out those refined feelings. Let us look for ways to serve others, and to teach our children that rather than Christmas being all about "What am I going to get," it can also be about "What am I going to give?" to help our children find true magic, to find God within.

May you have the very best *Season* ever, and in *magic and awe* may the tender and all-powerful Divine Incarnation of Christ be born in you.

November 30

God's Emissary

Mother Hamilton, India, 1977.**

have been spending a special amount of time focused on the transcripts of Mother's Talks as I work to put them into book form. As I do so, I am conscious of what a powerful engine she was for God. The other attribute that stands out for me is her willingness to share, from a human level, what her life was like.

Mother's life as a God-woman is perhaps unique because so many of her teachings about the inner meaning of the scriptures are taken from an intimate portrait of her life. Although Yoganandaji shared much about his life and his discipleship with his guru for all to see, Mother's experiences relate to a major shift of understanding about the life and teachings of Jesus the Christ; it affects all Christendom and beyond.

It is remarkable (as in a once-in-many lifetimes experience is remarkable) to be given work by Mother and Master, in whatever degree they have given us to help. No matter what role we play in the work, there is nothing insignificant in what we do. It is a ruse of the ego that makes us think that our lives do not matter, or at least do not matter much.

I think of Brother Lawrence washing dishes at the monastery. He was reputed to be not good at anything, so he was put on what was considered a lowly cleanup duty. Who the head of the monastery was at the time—I do not know. Who the bishop or even the pope was at the time—I do not know. But, through his letters in *The Practice of the Presence of God,* I know Brother Lawrence.

As you go about your life, you may sometimes believe that no one sees or cares about all that you do, but this is not the truth. This is especially true when you are making a sincere spiritual effort in your life. Because, by connecting your life with God's, you are unleashing a tremendous force for good in this world. The more deeply you are immersed in God, the greater the good being done.

There are no insignificant lives in this world, period. There are no exceptions to this. The original screenplay for "It's a Wonderful Life" was not about Jimmy Stewart's role as the bank CEO, rather the main role was played by a bank clerk. He was shown the world, by his guardian angel, as if he had never lived. Because he was not the bank clerk, another man had the job and embezzled money from the bank. The bank failed due to the theft and therefore a number of local businesses failed as well. The whole town and its economy suffered because this one man was not there to do his humble job honestly. Every life is important, and you are indispensable to the role you play; therefore, you must play it well.

By meditating regularly and deeply, you change not only your life, but your family's life, your community, and even the world at large. There is simply no way for you to accurately assess all the ways that your spiritual practice is absolutely needed by this world. Therefore, resolve that whatever role you are playing in this world, you play it well, and you enter into your spiritual practice with all of your heart, mind, and soul—for you are God's emissary.

December 6

A Most Excellent Result

Stained glass in the chapel
at Providence Hospital:
Gratitude to this great master.

We went in for my four-month CT/PET scan. When I told Carla I appreciated her coming (as she has been to every appointment and stayed in the room after each operation), she said, "Where else would I be!"

I am now familiar with the procedure for the PET/CT scan: a restrictive diet the day before, nothing to eat six hours before, all to make the body hungry for sugar. A concoction of a radium marker (which they assure me is mostly gone in a few hours) and sugar is injected and lights up areas of the body that absorb the sugar, and tumors love sugar, so if they are present, they light up during the scan.

The tech took three different pokes to get access to the blood system. I am told I am most difficult (having wiggly veins). He always talks for a good twenty minutes about his life (including pictures from his phone, as he is a special Ram edition!) before he gives me the radium, but eventually, we get there. For about an hour I rest (not even reading) as the marker circulates through my system, a wonderful meditation time.

Then later, a short walk into a room with a large machine in it. I lie down on a narrow platform, am strapped in, and asked not to move, and then I am conveyed into a four-foot deep tunnel with a few inches above me. Fortunately, I do not mind caves and enclosed spaces, in fact, I rather like them. Asked beforehand if I want music played, I decline, again, an excellent time to meditate; besides, my mind can reproduce any music I know with stunning quality. The machine whirs as I am shuffled forward and back, as it slowly scans up and down this body. After about an hour, I am taken out and then I reverse my direction on the platform and once again I enter the tube and more sound from the multimillion-dollar PET/CT machine, as it does what it does. Twenty minutes or so later, I am fully baked and am given a hand up as I emerge from the procedure.

Meanwhile, Carla went to the beautiful little chapel that is provided by the Providence Hospital, a hospital founded years ago by nuns, it continues to sport religious icons and prayers on walls throughout the buildings. Carla felt the wonderful support and presence of Mother Hamilton and the Masters while meditating there.

She then had the inspiration to call the doctor's office; I was not able to get an appointment until the end of December, a long time to wait for scan results. They tend not to give you the results until they see you in person. The weather has been turning cold and apparently, some cautious souls decided not to keep their appointments out of concern it might snow—we could see the doctor later that afternoon! Carla said to me that this was only the outward reason given for their cancellations; she knew it was God who made all the arrangements.

Normally, it takes 24 hours to have a specialist read the results of the scan, but the nurse put in a call, and when we met with the doctor that very afternoon, he had the results in hand. After waiting for the doctor (he usually runs generously behind schedule), he came in to say that the scan was clear, no evidence of tumors, a very happy outcome (the second scan now that has come back clean). One reason he is so far behind scheduled time is that once he is with us, it seems he has no other place to be, and we met with him for nearly an hour.

We review the scans, looking at the body as if from above the head, and with a movement of a mouse, we view the spine and internal organs up and down at various layers, as well as seeing the whole body from the front, and through many other different windows to the internal workings of the body. The brain, kidneys, colon, and liver all light up, as they readily absorb sugar. We can see the staples left by a previous surgery, a fascinating view of the internal body. My original surgeon, who seems to have taken over my case, is a saint—he has a positive, healing presence and brims with intelligence as well as perpetual curiosity. I think it unusual that a surgeon would continue as a primary doctor with me now, but Carla has the thought it is because he finds something in us that he likes (presumably more than my small intestines, liver, and gallbladder resections and removals!).

Afterward, we visit the chapel to give thanks and to be absorbed in His Presence. I tell God that I hope it is not due to attachment to the body that I feel this great joy, but He is bubbling up with blissfulness as we sit before His altar. I also thank so many of you who have sent prayers and notes of support and love. Science may have difficulty quantifying the effects of prayer, but I have no doubt whatsoever that you have been essential in this time of physical challenges and that my smooth recoveries from major surgeries and multiple procedures have been made possible by your loving support—**Thank You.** And, for the grace and love I feel from God and the Masters, there is no end to my gratitude. Surely, and not just for this, my life has been blessed and my soul melts in gratitude.

The only difficulty in what turned out to be a long day at the hospital is that the hours wore away and it became clear I would not be back in time for our Skype Service with the Ashland Group; I only hope they will forgive me for missing our time together, for what, I think, is for a good reason and a most excellent result.

December 9

Food for the Soul

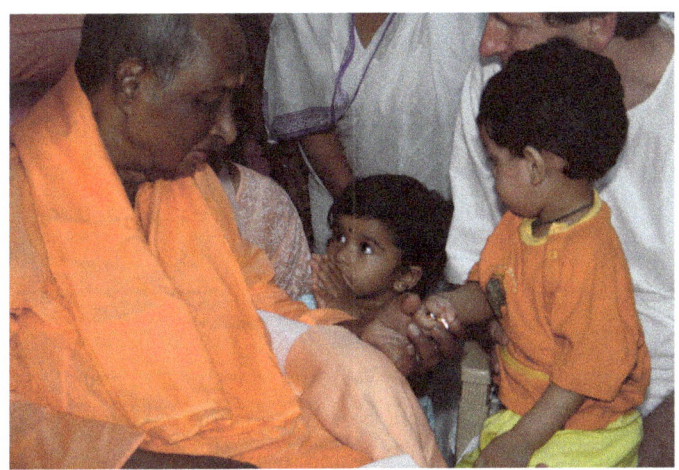

Swami Satchidananda gives prasad (blessed food)
to a little boy on Yogacharya David's lap, while a
little girl pronams to Swamiji, Anandashram, 2007.

O ur eating habits can teach us many valuable life-lessons about living in the world. Food is a powerful part of people's lives; our relationship with food is something we must encounter many times throughout the day. To find peaceful, healthful relations with food is not only good for the body, but also for the mind and soul as well.

Life-Lessons

When we eat to excess, we suffer the consequences: we feel uncomfortable afterward, it makes us lethargic; if done recurrently, it adds to our weight and ultimately, it makes us sick. Why do we do it then? Many times, we do not consider the consequences but are only caught up in the desire to eat more and more in the moment. The life-lesson: always consider the after-effect of any action you do. After-effects are much better indicators of the beneficence of any action than how it feels initially. There is a saying, when you are faced with a decision: do what is more difficult; it is usually the right choice.

Another lesson from our relationship with food is the fact that many of the foods we crave are the wrong foods for us to eat. It seems a betrayal of the body to want those things that are injurious rather than salubrious. A child may eat something sugary for the first time: the eyes light up, a smile erupts, and there is a request for more, please. Some people say they have a chocolate addiction; I say eat all you want, if it is sugar-free chocolate—there are few takers! When something is _too good_, it is likely <u>not good</u> for you. Oh, this body, simply _a nest of troubles!_ The life-lesson: be moderate—and be cautious of those things that feed desire nature.

In our modern world, products come in big packages and with great flair—meant to be consumed in extraordinary quantities. Super-sized packaging of food leads to super-sized bodies to match! Bigger is not better, certainly not better for you. Think about the actual size of your stomach and intestines, then think of how much we cram into them to be digested. It is truly amazing how much abuse our body endures, oftentimes without great complaint for many years. Life-lesson: rather than getting things because they are super-sized, because bigger is better—think about what the right-size is for you.

We can consume food without being conscious of tasting what we are eating, only taking mouthful after mouthful. To take in food with appreciation may sound like the opposite of what a spiritual person should do, but when you combine the consciousness of good taste and awareness of the high quality of the food, and sprinkle it with a keen gratitude to the Giver of life and all good things, then the act of eating is spiritualized. Life-lesson: be conscious of the beauty in your life with a spirit of gratitude to your Infinite Beloved—in this way, you appreciate and spiritualize all of life's activities.

With the Holidays in season, we can give "treats" to ourselves to the point of making the body sick. Hypocrites said, *let your medicine be food, and your food medicine.* Life lesson: let all the activities of your body, mind, and spirit be what is best and for the highest in you, and through the law of cause and effect, good things will come to you. What you give up in the moment can pay dividends in years to come. The law of reciprocity works for both the harmful things not done, as well as positive, thoughtful words and deeds that are done. I am sure you agree, meditation stands right at the top of that list of *treats,* through which you imbibe the highest quality food for the soul.

Make this season a true celebration of all that is good, beneficial, and uplifting. Treat yourself to the greatest gift in life: communion with God. In that, you may feast without limit with only good consequence. Learn life's lessons, be wise in all things, and find true happiness.

Yogacharya David holding prasad given
to honor Mother Hamilton's Mahasamadhi
Anniversary, Anandashram, 2007.

December 11

THE LOVE OF DIVINE MOTHER

*Adi Shakti, the Supreme Spirit without attributes***

Master Paramhansa Yogananda and Papa Ramdas both worshiped God as Divine Mother; Jesus and Mother Hamilton were more focused on God as Heavenly Father. Since God is both personal and impersonal, you may conceive of God in any way that draws you closer to Him.

There are those who relate most easily to Jesus, others to Krishna, and some relate to their teacher/guru—such as our own dear Mother. What is missing in the West, due to Jesus' and the Jewish tradition of focusing on Heavenly Father, is the part played by Divine Mother (even though the word Holy Ghost is feminine, still it does not tend to evoke that part of us that relates to sacred Mother). Although, for Catholics, Mother Mary is looked to for compassion and divine intercession.

Both Papa and Master felt that Divine Mother drew one closer than Father. A mother accepts her children more easily and unconditionally than a father—looking after the detailed needs of her dear ones. As Papa wandered as a penniless sadhu all over India, he had countless experiences of Divine Mother looking after him with such tender care. Whether it was providing what he needed for food, safety, or shelter, Divine Mother was so loving and protective of her dear child, Ramdas.

For Master, it was Divine Mother who drew him unto Herself. With the death of his mother when he was but a child, he deeply mourned for her—only increasing his ardor for finding the love of Divine Mother. Master Mahasaya, a great soul who was a disciple of the remarkable Ramakrishna Paramhansa, helped open the doorway for Master to get firsthand experience with the Divine Mother. He received Her blessed assurance that She had ever loved him, and it was She that he saw behind the eyes of his own mother.

Now, God made us in His likeness and Image, and that includes those aspects that are feminine as well as masculine. God loves to sport as those manifestations that delight us and draw us closer. So, Infinite Spirit expresses Itself in unlimited ways, and happily responds to our deepest yearnings. Here on earth, Divine Mother is a much-desired form that may manifest in any number of expressions in India, Quan Yin (Guanyin) in China, or numerous variations the world over, as Her expressiveness knows no limit.

In your spiritual journey, feel that God is looking after you as a solicitous mother would look after her child. Divine Mother is ever anxious that you be safe and comforted, that you know you have Her eternal love. Whatever you fill your mind with, you draw unto yourself. Feel the tenderness and love of Divine

Mother; have full awareness She is ever looking after you. Look into those soft, melting eyes and know She has ever loved you. Let Her solace ever make you know that you are Her child—that you are in Her, even as She is in you.

Note: I continue to be deeply indrawn; however, in the paradox of Spirit, I feel my closeness to you more than ever. Communing with the eternal One, let us know that we are ever joined in Divine union through our Heavenly Father, Divine Mother.

December 15

Freshly Born Truth

The third Super Moon over Saratoga Straights.

There are certain universal truths that, whether they are practiced or not, those with at least a modicum of intelligence and a reasonably good heart accept as true. Wisdom is usually simply put but reaches to the heart of the matter. Its breach of practice causes untold mischief in the world that leads to unnecessary suffering. One such truth is the Golden Rule: treat others as you wish to be treated. Perhaps there is no greater guide to good behavior than this. Imagine a world in which this rule is observed by one and all!

Then there is Swami Ramdas' creed of universal love and service. Putting into place this maxim brings hearts and minds together as they march toward the fulfillment of what humankind is really intended to be. Universal love and service is not a difficult idea to understand, only its practice requires self-mastery—your little self that leads you to anger, greed, and fear needs to be replaced with a pure perception—seeing that the world is God.

Jesus quoted ancient texts when he said that the greatest law is to *love the Lord thy God with all thy heart, mind, and strength,* and the second law, which is like the first, *to love thy neighbor as thy self.* Putting this into practice solves every human and spiritual problem of humanity and leads all to the kingdom of heaven.

Babaji said that *humility is pleasing to the Lord above all other qualities.* Lahiri Mahasaya said to *solve your problems through meditation; exchange unprofitable religious speculation for actual God-contact.* Sri Yukteswarji said to *forget the past, the vanished lives of all men are dark with many shames. Human conduct is ever unreliable until anchored in the Divine. Everything in the future will improve if you are making a spiritual effort now.* Master Paramhansa Yogananda poetically summarized his life of devotion and realization in the words, *God, God, God.* And Mother Hamilton encapsulated all spiritual practice with the teaching, *keep your mind on God.*

We really do know what we should do. As followers of this path, we have been given the highest, most powerful principles and techniques for spiritual evolution, for ourselves as well as for the world at large. It is up to each one of us to fulfill the vision that Jesus, Babaji, and all the masters have for us. We may not be able to force the world to be how we would like it, but we can change ourselves, and therefore be agents of change for others.

Let us put the universal truths we do know to work, not delay even for a moment. Meditation is a keystone, for it is in turning the mind inward that we touch the hem of God, and through that proximity, we are purified, and these universal truths then spontaneously live themselves through us. Thus, we find confirmed through our own experience, those truths we have sensed for so long are directly revealed by the Author of all life—and are freshly born in us.

December 18

Was It a Year Ago—Or a Lifetime Ago?

Yogacharya David in Boise, Idaho, September, 2015.**

Just a year ago I had been diagnosed with melanoma that had traveled to the small intestines and was thought to be in some of the lymph nodes; I had an operation that removed part of the small intestines and was still quite weak from the previous internal blood loss. A little later in the year, I was to visit the hospital again for a resection of the liver due to more melanoma, and the removal of the gallbladder. These have been interesting times!

Thanks to modern medicine, these tumors were removed, but I am sure this would have been a death sentence in times past when less advanced medical science was available. And thanks to the many prayers and powerful thoughts of so many wonderful souls, my recovery was quick, smooth, and complete.

Last night, we had our annual Christmas carols at Jill and Greg's; a year ago on the same day, I was just being taken by wheelchair to the door of the hospital and into the car for Carla to drive back to Camano. Was that a year ago—or was that another lifetime ago? The memory seems like a dream from the night that loses validity with the dawning of the day.

Today, I feel very well. Today there is no sign of disease. With firm instructions to this body to effectively fight off any future ungoverned growths! Today God is fully present, even as He has been throughout this past year. I truly feel that one of the effects of your prayers and the spiritual work we do is that there is no leave-over, no clinging emotional charges from the events of the past year.

One of the blessings and the curses of the intelligence God has given us as human beings is that we can anticipate future events as well as remember past events as if they are occurring in the moment. If these are useful or pleasant anticipations or memories, then they are blessings. However, if they are not useful and are unpleasant, then this faculty of mind becomes a curse. In body memory, such as Post Traumatic Stress Disorder (PTSD), nightmarish dreams, or in waking daydreams, these daemons of thought can make life a living hell.

A product of realizing God is to naturally live in the moment. The past is a river whose waters have flowed by and returned to the ocean—something to be remembered, but now given back to God. The future is in the Infinite's hands, and if there are concerns for what may come, then faith, trust, and reliance upon the Supreme bring peace in the moment.

So, in celebration of this sacred season, we gathered together to sing Christmas carols, so many beautiful and favorite songs that are kept in a special treasure box to be opened and enjoyed only at this time of year. So many loving dear friends all come together, with delicious treats to taste and warmth and love to share. This morning, there is a dusting of white snow covering everything as if the world is wrapped in snowy gift wrap. Later, we will have our Christmas Service, and there will be more invocations for God-consciousness to be part of everyone's awareness—for peace on earth, and goodwill toward all humankind.

So, if you are here, a part of these wonderful, sacred events, or if you are in distant places, I earnestly wish you peace, an inner assurance that God is with you and guiding you, and that you feel the warmth and love of association that God effortlessly connects us all, wherever we may be, anywhere around this globe, or beyond.

December 22

ATTAINING NEEDED VELOCITY

Paramhansa Yogananda attained the
needed velocity! Flowers by Rebecca H.

The after-effect of this past weekend of Christmas celebration continues to be with me. The feeling of warmth, love, and delight at coming together: caroling at Christmas, communion with our Beloved, friendship, and a delectable potluck—all combined to be a feast for the soul.

Certainly, devotees coming together in Satsang to commune with Truth, the eternal Being, is of tremendous help to our spiritual practice. Traditionally, this is done when we come together as a group to focus upon God alone. However, the inner meaning of Satsang is fulfilled anytime we are merged in God; then there is association through oneness with Sat: the great *I AM*.

How to describe what *living in Him, and He in me,* is like? There is only He, the Divine Consciousness that is the eternal Substance, all power, and all intelligence—everything there is!

I do remember my life before living in Him, I remember the pain of being separate from God. Also, through my sadhana years, I know the times of being with God alternating with the loss of connection with Him. To be in continuous communion with the Divine is categorically different from those previous states, a type of quantum leap. It is important that we keep the Goal of goals in the forefront, so that we do not stop short of experiencing Him deeply and continuously.

When Master was told by his guru that he had discovered God, Yogananda protested that he did not think that he had. Sri Yukteswarji went straight to the heart of the confusion: *God-realization is not the attainment of miraculous powers—it is ever-new joy.* We all love to have God come in super-ordinary ways, but really, miracles are *small potatoes* compared to exploring His vast Being. The real touchstone of God-experience is blissful joy.

How to add velocity to your spiritual practice so that you may fully realize the Divine Presence within and without? We have been given the very best tools to gain the highest consciousness: Kriya yoga meditation, chanting, keeping our mind on God, serving Him in all we do and in whom all we meet, and divinely loving Him are all-inclusive and propel us to ultimate fulfillment as a modern house-holder yogi.

I have had nothing but glowing admiration for Babaji's Kriya Yoga as taught by Master—with the perspective of over 40 years of practice since my initiation by my blessed Guru. I know of no other practice that works so directly with the spine and the brain for the evolution of all three bodies: the physical, astral, and causal. The deeper we go in our practice, the more profound are the changes that occur in the subtle spine through breath, focus of mind, and transformative life-energy. We are truly blessed for the intelligent design that has gone into this practice and provides for perfect balance.

To accelerate all areas of our spiritual practice, we must hone our ability to focus on the Goal. Two great drivers in my sadhana were the need to know the truth, and, to experience bliss; these were not just casual ideas, but were constant needs that rendered all other desires distantly archaic. To add propellant to our aspiration for God, **we must have a compelling aspect of God that we cannot live without.**

To break out of the earth's gravity, a rocket must attain the speed of 25,000 miles per hour. To break the gravity of earthly attachment, we must necessarily travel at the speed of God! Which can only be attained by His booster rocket of Grace. We draw Grace to ourselves when we *love the Lord thy God with all our heart, mind, strength, and soul.* To attain the velocity we need by finding that part of God, we must have the desire for God beyond all other desires. Then, He cannot stay away, but will be drawn irresistibly by the magnet of our love—we then break free of earthly bonds and float free in His truth and His bliss.

December 24

The Eve of Christmas

Nativity in Shepherd Field Chapel.**

ave a blessed Christmas Eve. It is a remarkable time, for many it includes family; for all of us, it is a time to tune into the Divine emanations resounding within and without. It is touching to think about that historical night when Mother Mary suffered while traveling on a donkey or walking on foot as they made their way to Bethlehem. Then, to find no room available. In those days, it was not an inn as we think of it, but a walled enclosure, open to the sky overhead. However, even these were filled to overflowing. But kindness won out as they were directed to a cave used as a barn. The humble beginnings of God born in man: a cave so entirely appropriate for a Yogi-Christ.

It is also entirely fitting to meditate upon the inner drama of God born in man. While it is true that all humankind has the Christ-seed within, for most of humanity it lies in potential only.

For aspiring souls that seed awakens, sending out branches to the Light, roots deep into the Soul. It is the *tree of life* that is growing right within us! New growth captures new Light, new revelations, and ever-new bliss. This is humankind's next evolutionary step; it occurs within the devoted individual, and as more individuals burst open the shell of humanness, a forest of Christ-like souls will inhabit this earth—bringing a new era of peace and fulfilling humankind's greatest potential. What we celebrate tonight is the tremendous potential embedded in you, in me, and in all. This is the eve on which it all begins.

December 25

CHRISTMAS MORN'

Yogacharya David and Carla's mantle with
portrait of Mother Hamilton and decorations.

These early Christmas hours feel very sacred, the air vibrating with *Aumen*—a celestial song of the Infinite. The Christmas tree lit, and tiny lights all around the crèche scene on the fireplace mantel.

As I stand and gaze at the images of the dear holy family, I touch the feet of the blessed baby Jesus. A thrill of Divine Presence captures my soul. A powerful surge thrills throughout every cell of my body. I stand enraptured for some time. Then my attention is drawn to the Holy Mother, and compassion for what she must have gone through humanly, the strain and stress of traveling when so fully pregnant, the uncertainties she had faced, the surrender of her soul, the handmaiden of God—all come flooding into me.

Gradually, my attention swings to Joseph, again on a human level: the sense of family responsibility and the uncertainties. His intuition told him his soon-to-be wife was pure. His intuition would take the little family to far away Egypt to protect them, and tell him when it was safe to return. A man of strength, courage, conviction, and perfect faith.

Then I looked at the angel blowing her horn in celebration, in joy resounding sounds of bliss! Yes, a night to celebrate, *God with us!* And the wise men, certainly saints, and sages, all—men of transcendent vision. They bow at the feet of a baby, in perfect submission to the Divine child. And the shepherd boy, coming without the understanding of the wise men, but in the simplicity of childlike love and faith. All have a place in this pageant of Light and Love come to the world, the redeemer of humankind and a blessing to all.

Then my vision is drawn to the picture of Mother Hamilton, looking at the holy scene as from above. Born on Christmas day, a birthdate-harbinger for the life she was to live—a Christ-like life. She too would suffer, not be understood, would strive for, and be loyal to God to the very end. A lover of Truth, and a servant of her Guru through thick and thin. That life is now over, Mother, and now you reside in the great heavens, serving all, even as you served on earth. Happy Birthday, Mother! I surrender at your feet.

And you, my dear Ones, may you also feel this warmth of love and sacredness of Christmas: a happy day filled with Divine remembrance and wonder-filled activities.

With all love and blessings,
DAVID

December 27

Papa's Sannyas

Swami Ramdas: A perfect flower of full God-realization.

On a Wednesday night in March 1974, I met Mother Hamilton. In addition to the tremendous talk she gave that evening, she also led us in chanting Ram Nam. I found Mother's tune haunting but unforgettable and found myself singing it after meeting her. When I chanted Om Sri Ram Jai Ram Jai Jai Ram (Victory to God), it started a vibrational feeling, something powerful and uplifting that soon gave me peace and bliss.

It took some time before I came to know details of Swami Ramdas, first from Mother's talks describing her time with him, her reading from the Vision Magazine most every talk, then finally

when I read his books. In 1979, Mother announced the new publication of *The Gospel of Swami Ramdas,* which included gener-
ous excerpts of Mother's and Papa's (Swami Ramdas) talks from
1957. It was obvious what a powerhouse of God Papa was; he
started Mother into the *Mystical Crucifixion;* it was he and Master
Paramhansa Yogananda who spiritually protected her all the way
to her full God-realization.

I found every written word from Papa was saturated with truth
and wisdom and his words lifted me closer to the goal. The Ram
Nam chant continued in me down through the years as an essential part of my spiritual practice. I did not have a voice that could
sing for very long, so after a few repetitions verbally I switched to
mental chanting; it was not till later that I read that Papa recommended mental chanting, saying it was more powerful. Papa grew
into an absolute fixture in my life. His Ram Nam chant, his perfectly expressed wisdom, humor, openness, love of God and God
in humanity were, and are, inspiring beyond mere words. How
blessed I am to have him in my life.

December 27, we celebrate Papa's Sannyas Day—the day he
put on the orange swami clothes (as Ram willed him to do), and
committed himself to the life of a wandering sadhu with the new
name of Swami Ramdas—meaning *servant of God.* With that inau-
guration came a great movement of love of God and perfect surrender to Him into the world. Papa very rarely recommended the
sannyas life to others; what he wants for all aspirants is perfect
surrender and non-attachment to things of the world. As Papa
said, "Sannyas is principally a state of internal detachment to the
objects of the senses. The external garb is only a symbol of inner
transformation."

The simplest means to have non-attachment is to have a total
focus on, and surrender to, God—by making Him first in your
heart, mind, and soul. Be a faithful lover of God: chant His name
all the hours of the day, feel His bliss surging throughout your

entire being, and you will be His, and He will be yours. Non-attachment to this world and perfect comprehension of the universal vision of God make for pure happiness no matter your situation. Whatever color clothes you wear, you will then have the orange flame of renunciation burning brightly within you; you will be purified, so that within and without there is nothing but Ram. By striving for and attaining this exalted state, you perfectly honor Papa's Sannyas Day.

> Mere external renunciation is of no avail . . . To assume Sannyas in the hope that by taking merely that step you would realize God, is perfectly wrong . . . Sannyas is not a thing to be received from, or given to, anybody. It is a dedication of our entire being to the Lord and His service. It is a spontaneous wave of aspiration rising from within our own heart.
>
> —Swami Ramdas

December 31

UNWRITTEN PAGES OF THE NEW YEAR

Lakshmi, Goddess of Prosperity and Harmony,
with Ganesh, God of Wisdom and Overcomer
of Obstacles, ushering you into the New Year.**

A s I think of this coming new year, I picture opening a new book, or a fresh unmarked page upon which to write, perhaps sitting in a theater waiting for a performance to begin. There is openness, a hushed expectation, curiosity, and a desire to know what the supreme Author will scribe, say, or do in our life. The start of anything can seem exciting, tenuous, and uncertain, all at the same time.

Through the years, we can become over-familiar with life, and in doing so, we lose many precious qualities: becoming dulled to life's wonders, entrenched in sameness, hypnotized by fear, lack, self-condemnation, or enmeshed in bitterness. These are life-killing tendencies, and they suck the joy right out of us. These perspectives are simply states of mind, as demonstrated by the fact that the person next to us with very similar circumstances can have a completely different and elevated attitude.

The very root of this universe is Ananda; it is an explosion of joyful-bliss. And life, when lived in God, is filled with Divine Presence. No matter how far we wander from our Source, it never stops being the essence of who and what we are; this is a fact. It has been a source of great mischief that religious leaders invented eternal hell and damnation. Reason tells us that God, being the creator of all, and who is more loving than the most devoted parent, will never abandon His children, never! We are made in His likeness and His image. Therefore, we are eternally His.

The real question, then, is how to consciously re-establish that connection? For that, we have been given the truth by living spiritual masters, and we have received the means to practice the very highest methods for realizing God by our Guru-lineage. Mental speculation is but a vague shadow compared to the light of realization. To step into that light, we must strive with all of our might; with great courage, we must step out of the shadows and be illumined.

Sri Yukteswarji assured us that all of us have had a trail of misdeeds littered behind us, but that should not stop us from striving for Self-realization. But, neither will spiritual laziness get us to the Goal. I have devotees tell me that they have no time for meditation because they play golf each morning; some wish to drink alcohol or use drugs; others are driven by the need to socialize with friends, watch television, or surf the net—there are a million excuses. But there is one compelling reason for knowing God—it is only through oneness with Him that we can have lasting happiness, a fulfillment that does not diminish with time nor is it severed by death.

As aspirants, we continue to live in the body—in this world. As such, there are things we must have for the survival of this body: clothing, shelter, and food; at times, we need medical care; for many who have taken on the responsibilities of family, the list grows longer. So, we work to have balance in our lives—there are legitimate desires to fulfill living in this material realm. For some, it is completing education, excelling in a profession, building a business, or raising a family. Looking to the new year, we can take into account the many aspects of life—material as well as spiritual.

Create a clear picture of who you want to be and what you want to accomplish—for every creation begins with an idea. Putting yourself into that picture, feel what that is like: the sense of self-mastery, the balance, peace, bliss, wisdom, the whole package. Think also of accomplishing what you have come to do in this world: for example, service to humanity and the fulfillment of your dreams. Expand your consciousness to comfortably and easily accommodate your dreams—definitely invite God in to be a co-creator with you. Remember, you are made in His likeness and His image; there are no limits to what He can do through you.

Blessings, blessings for the unwritten pages that will be filled with the unfolding days of this new year, and that you be a perfect conduit for the supreme Light of this world to manifest through your every thought, word, and action.

Conclusion

PRAYER

Spontaneously, my soul silently cried,
"Oh my Lord, Oh my Lord," again and again.

I was nothing. He is everything.

"Oh my Lord."

After some time, an inner question came from the
all-pervasive Christ Consciousness: "What do you pray for?"

The thought flashed for my health,
but I discarded that instantly,

"Oh my Lord, I pray for this world.

You are all-powerful, You are everywhere
present, awaken Yourself in all humanity.

You are the Great Awakener,

You are the eternal Light, You are the great
Awakener, awaken Yourself in all humanity."

And so went my prayer out of the depths of my soul.[10]

—YOGACHARYA DAVID

OM TAT SAT AUM

---

10   This prayer is from Yogacharya David's September 30, 2016 discourse.

Mount Temple, Alberta, Canada, painting by Dennis Brown.

References

Brother Lawrence. (2010). *The Practice of the Presence of God.* New York: Paraclete Press.

Hickenbottom, Yogacharya David. (2022). *Silence: Entering the Cosmic Sea of Consciousness.* Camano Island, WA.: The Cross and The Lotus Publishing.

Muggeridge, Malcolm. (1971). *Something Beautiful for God.* New York: Harper Collins.

Paramhansa Yogananda. (1995). *God Talks with Arjuna: Bhagavad Gita.* Los Angeles, CA.: Self-Realization Fellowship.

Paramhansa Yogananda. (1946). *Autobiography of a Yogi.* New York: The Philosophical Library.

Swami Satchidananda. (1979). *The Gospel of Swami Ramdas.* Bombay, India: For Anandashram by Bharatiya Vidya Bhavan.

Bible References

King James Bible Online: https//www.kingjamesbibleonline.org

Film References

A Christmas Carol, later released as *Scrooge*. (1951). George Minter Productions. Directed by Brian Desmond Hurst.

It's a Wonderful Life. (1946). Liberty Films. Directed by Frank Capra.

Jesus of Nazareth. (1977). ITC Entertainment, RAI. Directed by Franco Zeffirelli.

Website References

Mother Hamilton's quote reference: The Cross and The Lotus Publishing: www.crossandlotus.com

Yogacharya David's original discourse reference: www.crossandlotus.com

Anandashram reference: www.anandashram.org

Kahlil Gibran. *The Prophet*. On Work. www.goodreads.com

Ralph Waldo Emerson. *Essays: First Series*. (1841). Compensation. www.emersoncentral.com

William Arthur Ward quote on Gratitude: www.goodreads.com/quotes/421800

Image Attribution

With the exception of those listed below, all images are used courtesy of the David and Carla Hickenbottom portfolio. Photos were taken by David and Carla Hickenbottom or gifted with permission by friends, family, and devotees. Attribution for images from these sources has not been included here. Images of devotees or written submissions from devotees are all included after receiving consent for this book series. Images are either paid for or for free use in the public domain, Creative Commons licensing, or from other sources as noted.

January 03. *Hands Forming a Heart Shape* by Warmcolors on Dreamstime.com. License purchased.

January 05. Paramhansa Yogananda with his *Autobiography of a Yogi*. Commons.wikimedia.org. Public domain.

January 29. *Change* by Gunnar 3000 on Dreamstime.com. License purchased.

February 07. *Krishna Dancing on the Head of Kaliya*. India bazaar art, unknown author, c. 1950s. Commons.wikimedia.org. Public domain.

March 20. *Christ in Gethsemane* by Heinrich Hofmann, 1886. Commons.wikimedia.org. Public domain.

March 25. *Full Moon Over Clouds During Nighttime,* photo by Silas Van Overeem on Unsplash.com. Free use under the Unsplash license.

March 27. *Empty Tomb/Brown Rock Formation During Daytime*, photo by Pisit Heng on Unsplash.com. Free use under the Unsplash license.

April 09. Sri Yukteswar with Paramhansa Yogananda, Calcutta, 1935. *Autobiography of a Yogi*, p. 459. Commons.wikimedia.org. Public domain.

April 21. *Road to the Sky* by Levgenii Tryfonov on Dreamstime. com. License purchased.

May 08. Indian Goddess *Durga Ma* by krhm73 on Shutterstock. com. License purchased.

May 22. *Water Flowing Over Rocks* by Tyler Strange on Dreamstime.com. License purchased.

June 02. Ralph Waldo Emerson, 1857, by Josiah Johnson Hawes, print from 1880. Commons.wikimedia.org. Public domain.

June 09. *Alfter Kirche* Interior of St. Matthaus by Prof. Emeritus Hans Schneider is licensed under Creative Commons Attribution 4.0 International CC-BY 4.0 and Gnu Free Documentation License. Commons.wikimedia.org.

June 18. *Sacred Lotus Nelumbo Nucifera* by T. Voekler is licensed under Creative Commons CC-SA 3.0. Commons.wikimedia.org.

June 26. Sacagawea Birthplace in Salmon, Idaho (cropped) by Rickmouser45 is licensed under Creative Commons CC-BY-SA 4.0. Commons.wikimedia.org.

July 31. *Srimad Guru Adi Shankaracharya* by Raja Ravi Varma, c. 1904. Commons.wikimedia.org. Public domain.

August 03. Lahiri Mahasaya. *Autobiography of a Yogi*, p. 317. Commons.wikimedia.org. Public domain.

August 08. *Jesus Healing the Sick* by L. Caracciolo, 1927. Copy of the original artwork by Johann Heinrich Hofmann, c. 1890. Commons.wikimedia.org. Public domain.

August 12. *Krishna Shows Arjuna His Universal Form*. India bazaar art by C. Konddiah Raja c. 1950s. Wikipedia. Public domain.

August 21. *Hands Holding World* by Stephen Denness on Dreamstime.com. License purchased.

August 24. *Renaissance Fountain* by Csaba Peterdi on Dreamstime.com. License purchased.

August 28. *Himalaya Highways* by Steve Evans is licensed under Creative Commons CC BY 2.0. Commons.wikimedia.org.

August 31. *Elephant Balancing on a Colorful Ball* by Tsung-lin Wu on Dreamstime.com. License purchased.

October 28. *Krishna Tells (the) Gita to Arjuna* by Mahavir Prasad Mishra. Mahabharata: Tej Kumar Book Depot. Commons.wikimedia.org. Public domain.

November 02. Shiva statue *Kailash Nath Temple, Murugeshpalya, Bangalore* by Rameshng at Malayalam. Licensed under Creative Commons CC-BY-SA 3.0. Commons.wikimedia.org.

December 11. *Adi Shakti, the Supreme Spirit without attributes* by Soumik Barua is licensed under Creative Commons CC-BY-SA 4.0. Commons.wikimedia.org.

December 24. *Fresco in Shepherd Field Chapel* by Meunierd on Dreamstime.com. License purchased.

December 31. *Lakshmi Ganesh,* Tamil Cipart-521708 on Clker.com. Public domain. Cropped from original image.

Conclusion: *Mount Temple,* Alberta, Canada. Painting by Dennis Brown. Permission Granted.

Acknowledgments

Yogacharya David has a unique ability to share spiritual teachings and soul-enhancing reflections in a most accessible manner—he can reach us in our day-to-day ways of being as we strive to live a purposeful life. He guides us, and, even as he laughs at himself, he still seriously advocates for a wake-up process.

It is a privilege to form what we call Team-David, a dedicated team of aspirants who willingly devote time and expertise to ensuring that Yogacharya David's legacy of teachings reaches those who long for a deeper, broader, disciplined-yet-freeing approach to life's journey.

Carla Hickenbottom, David's wife and senior disciple, has been a major support throughout the preparation and publication process. Her loving oversight and her diligence as director of The Cross and The Lotus Publishing support us each step of the way.

Rebecca Harvey has been a major ongoing link to data collection and historical document searches. She seems to know just where to find more information on most everything we need. Her keen eye also provides an astute read that catches the forever-escaping grammatical challenges. Mira Lutz, our other Team-David member for the Discourses, has an excellent knowledge of grammar. It is a gift of Grace to have such a fine team working to prepare and publish Yogacharya David's series of six Discourse volumes.

Our team also includes my editor, Zia Cole, for all of the Discourse volumes—our gratitude to her for her astute eye and professional expertise.

Jan Westendorp of Kato Design and Photo brings her artistic and professional book-design expertise forward when working on our manuscripts. She provides us with elegant page layouts and image-refinement support, and in so many other ways, she has helped us create a beautiful series of six volumes.

Team-David feels that Yogacharya David would be delighted to know that his unique writings and teachings are available in book form for all who seek a deeper, sacred understanding of the human condition.

About the Author

Yogacharya David Hickenbottom (1954–2019) met his guru Yogacharya Mother Hamilton, a disciple of Paramhansa Yogananda, when he was a youth of 20. Yogacharya David became a Reverend in 1984. Mother Hamilton bestowed the Yogacharya title to David before she left her body in 1991.

The great Kriya Yoga lineage of India that came through Jesus, Babaji, Lahiri Mahasaya, and Sri Yukteswar to Yogananda, and then to Mother Hamilton, provides pathways to an appreciation of, and a faith in, the everyday sacred, to an understanding of higher dimensional wisdom, to an integral intuitive knowing of spiritual truths, and to the vibratory realms that permeate all that is, was, and will be.

Yogacharya David says: "An inner pain brought me to the path most unwillingly, and this inner pain kept me on the path. I put my shoulder to the wheel." He faced the crux of the spiritual dilemma—how to shift from the ego-driven lower or smaller human nature to a larger and luminous existence, intuitively attuned to our deeper and broader—vast—spiritual nature, thereby discovering the Living Truth. With this intense striving for Truth and Bliss, and with his Guru's Grace, David was carried through many years of Mystical Crucifixion spiritual experiences. His year in silence (2000–2001) established an inner state of stillness that never left him—ultimately contributing to his full Self-realization.

Also by Yogacharya David

2013–2019 Discourse Series:

- *Discourses—Volume One: 2013–14: Living a Spiritually Rich Life*

- *Discourses—Volume Two: 2015: Re-Union of Soul and Spirit*

- *Discourses—Volume Three: 2016: A True New Birth*

- *Discourses—Volume Four: 2017: Gateway to the Infinite*

- *Discourses—Volume Five: 2018: Standing on the Threshold of Eternity*

- *Discourses—Volume Six: 2019: Writing in the Book of Life*

Hickenbottom, Yogacharya David. (2022). *Touching the Supreme Spirit*. Infinite Calendar. Camano Island, WA.: The Cross and The Lotus Publishing.

Hickenbottom, Yogacharya David. (2022). *Silence: Entering the Cosmic Sea of Consciousness*. Camano Island, WA.: The Cross and The Lotus Publishing.

Hickenbottom, Yogacharya David. (2022). *Notes to Sadhakas*. Camano Island, WA.: The Cross and The Lotus Publishing.

Hickenbottom, Yogacharya David. (2021). *Climbing the Sacred Mountain: Poems and Prayers of a Western Yogi*. Camano Island, WA.: The Cross and The Lotus Publishing.

Hickenbottom, Yogacharya David. (2019). *My Spiritual India*. Camano Island, WA.: The Cross and The Lotus Publishing.